EDA TOPLISS and BRYAN GOULD

A Charter for the Disabled

Basil Blackwell &
Martin Robertson

© Eda Topliss and Bryan Gould 1981

First published in 1981 by Basil Blackwell Ltd
and Martin Robertson & Co. Ltd
108 Cowley Road, Oxford OX4 1JF, England

British Library Cataloguing in Publication Data

Topliss, Eda

  A charter for the disabled. — (Aspects of social policy series).
  1. Great Britain — Laws, statutes, etc.
  (Individual titles). *Chronically Sick and Disabled Persons Act 1970*
  2. Chronically ill — Great Britain
  3. Physically handicapped — Law and legislation — Great Britain
  I. Title   II Gould, Bryan   III. Series
  344' .41'03213   'KD3313

  ISBN 0 631 12833 6 ✓
  ISBN 0 631 12748 8 Pbk

Typesetting by The Drawing Room, Ashford, Middlesex.
Printed and Bound in Great Britain by Book Plan, Worcester

Contents

Contents

Acknowledgements

The authors wish to thank the Rt Hon. Alfred Morris MP for his encouragement and help in obtaining material for this book. Bryan Gould also gratefully acknowledges the assistance given to him by Kay Andrews of the House of Commons Library, and thanks Mrs. Gillian Gould for typing his part of the book. The views expressed in the book and any defects or omissions, are, however, entirely the responsibility of the authors.

The Chronically Sick and Disabled Persons Bill and the Chronically Sick and Disabled Persons Act 1970 are reproduced with the permission of the Controller of Her Majesty's Stationery Office.

Acknowledgements

The author wishes to thank...

CHAPTER ONE

The Background and Birth of the Chronically Sick and Disabled Persons Bill

As the Chronically Sick and Disabled Persons Bill completed its passage through the House of Lords, Lord Longford, who had taken responsibility for the Bill in the Upper House, declared that the Bill 'will always be associated with its creator, Mr Alf Morris'[1]. Lord Longford's remark was apt; private Members' Bills are, of course, always regarded as the creations of their sponsors, but this was more than usually true in the case of Alf Morris and the Chronically Sick and Disabled Persons Act 1970. It was in his profound interest in the problems of disablement that the Bill originated; it was his tact and skill that put and held together the team that drafted the Bill and carried it through all its parliamentary stages; and it was his political acumen and perseverance that ensured that the Bill reached the Statute Book before the guillotine imposed by an imminent General Election finally fell.

Alf Morris was a relatively new and inexperienced backbencher when he found himself confronted, in November 1969, with the challenge presented by coming first in the ballot for private Members' Bills. He had entered Parliament as the Member for the Manchester constituency of Wythenshawe in November 1964. He had already shown himself to be an active constituency Member and had become Parliamentary Private Secretary to Fred Peart, the Minister of Agriculture. His tenure of this unpaid office had been brought to an end when he was sacked, on the Prime Minister's instructions, for failing to support the Government on the question of whether Britain should enter negotiations for membership of the European Economic Community.

1

One of the main themes of Alf Morris's Parliamentary career had been his interest in disablement. This interest was more than merely academic or political in nature; it stemmed from a close personal acquaintance with the overwhelming difficulties that disabled people face. Alf Morris's father had been severely wounded during the First World War. His work as a signwriter had frequently been interrupted by bouts of illness as a result of his war wounds, which ranged from severe leg injuries to partial blindness. In the years before his death he had contracted tuberculosis, an all too familiar culmination of the cycle of illness and poverty, and it was this illness that eventually caused his death in 1935, when Alf Morris was only seven years old.

Alf Morris has recounted elsewhere[2] the problems of bureaucratic insensitivity and inadequate financial provision which his widowed mother faced following his father's death. He retained a vivid memory of the battles which had to be fought in order to establish his mother's status as a war widow and therefore her entitlement to a war widow's pension. As with so many other provisions in the Chronically Sick and Disabled Persons Act, Section 23, which simplifies the provisions for claiming war pensions, owes much to Alf Morris's personal knowledge and experience.

Alf Morris learned as a young child that the problems of the disabled – the unemployment, the poverty, the social restrictions – inevitably affect the whole family. These lessons were reinforced when he married in 1950 and went to live at the home of his wife's parents, both of whom were severely disabled. His mother-in-law was totally incapacitated by rheumatoid arthritis and was confined to a wheelchair. His father-in-law suffered from chronic bronchitis and died in a hospital ward in 1951. The housing conditions which Alf Morris and his wife shared with her parents can be regarded as the mainspring of those provisions in the Chronically Sick and Disabled Persons Act which oblige local housing authorities to make special provision for the housing needs of the disabled.

Alf Morris had left school at the age of fourteen, but in 1950, after a spell in the army, he secured a place to read Modern History at Oxford University. As well as extending his educational horizons, he was also developing an interest in politics. He became involved in both the Labour Party and the Co-operative Party, and the first speech he made as a delegate to the Co-operative Party's

Annual Conference was on the subject of the problems facing the disabled. By the time he followed his elder brother, Charles, into the House of Commons in 1964, a heavy burden of casework had made him familiar with the difficulties encountered by disabled people in large cities like Liverpool and Manchester.

As a Member of Parliament, Alf Morris had little choice but to pursue his interest in disablement. Any good constituency Member who provides a regular and effective service to his constituents will inevitably find that he is involved in the financial, housing and social problems of disabled people. As well as taking up constituency cases with officialdom and with Ministers, Alf Morris was also active in the House of Commons itself. In the period between 1964 and 1969 he asked dozens of questions on the problems of the disabled and spoke in a number of debates (usually those initiated by other backbenchers) on similar topics.

Many of the provisions of the Chronically Sick and Disabled Persons Act have their origin in the questions Alf Morris asked during this period. A recurring theme was his insistence that too little was known about the number of disabled people in society. He asked questions about the establishment of a register of disabled people[3] and about the number of young people who were chronically ill.[4] He was also concerned at the way in which young people who were crippled as a result of motor accidents were treated in geriatric wards.[5]

A number of his questions referred to the problems which disabled people face in moving around and in obtaining access to public buildings. He asked, for example, about the number of public lavatories in Manchester which were accessible to people in wheelchairs,[6] and he was also concerned about the progress of a Manchester experiment which provided telephones for the elderly and the housebound.[7] On several occasions he asked questions about or participated in debates concerning mentally handicapped children.[8] With this record of concern, interest and expertise established, it was not surprising that he should think of legislating in this field when he won the ballot for private Members' Bills.

The legislative field into which he ventured was not over-burdened. There was very little statute law which dealt specifically with the problems of disabled people. The Blind Persons Act 1920, had been introduced after the First World War to provide instructional facilities for disabled ex-servicemen and the Second

World War similarly prompted the Disabled Persons (Employment) Act 1944, whose object was to provide industrial retraining and rehabilitation for disabled people. This Act also provided for a register of disabled people and required employers of any size to employ a quota of 3 per cent of disabled people in their work force. This provision has been widely ignored by many employers, including Government departments, and little attempt is made to enforce it, a sad commentary on the seriousness of purpose with which Governments have approached these issues. The only other important legislative intervention had been the Disabled Persons (Employment) Act 1958, which encouraged the expansion of sheltered workshops for disabled people.

Disabled people were, of course, to some extent beneficiaries of the National Insurance and Social Security schemes set up in Britain after the Second World War. While the National Assistance scheme (later to become the Supplementary Benefit scheme) constituted a sort of safety net for all members of society, including the disabled, it provided for a level of support defined in terms of short-term subsistence and did not grapple in any real sense with the particular problems of the disabled. The disabled also found that they were excluded, in most cases, from the more generous provisions of the National Insurance Scheme, since most of them had no record of employment and therefore had not paid the contributions needed to entitle them to benefits.

As a result of these deficiencies, a number of voluntary organizations representing the disabled had become active. The Disablement Income Group, for example, had been formed in order to press for an income to be available to disabled people as of right. But the disabled were still an under-represented and ill-organized sector of society, and their problems were only dimly perceived by the public and by politicians.

Before Alf Morris became a Member of Parliament in 1964 disablement had simply not figured on the parliamentary agenda at all. There had been no mention of the problems of the disabled in either of the major party manifestos, and there had been no debate on disablement in the whole of the parliamentary term from 1959 to 1964. Gradually, however, the climate had begun to change. The activities of the Disablement Income Group, the Central Council for the Disabled, the National Campaign for the Young Chronic Sick, the Disabled Living Foundation and other voluntary organizations had gradually raised the level of interest. Alf Morris and other backbench Members of Parliament, such as the Conservative John Astor and Alf Morris's Labour colleague Jack Ashley, showed an increasing interest in questions affecting the disabled.

The legislative and institutional background was changing as well. The Seebohm Committee had produced a major report[9] on the social services, which presaged a fundamental reorganization; a substantial section of the report dealt with the needs of physically and mentally handicapped people. Legislation to implement the Committee's recommendations was promised, and the Government was also working on a Green Paper dealing with the reorganization of the National Health Service.

The Department of Health and Social Security, under the guidance of the Secretary of State, Richard Crossman, was preparing a massive National Superannuation and Social Insurance Bill which, among other things, would provide for the first time an attendance allowance for disabled people and an earnings-related invalidity pension.

Of equal importance to the disabled, the Government had somewhat belatedly recognized the need to establish the dimensions of disablement in Britain. In a written reply to a Parliamentary Question on 23rd October 1967,[10] the Minister of Health announced that a major survey would be undertaken whose object would be to assess the number of disabled people in the country. By the time Alf Morris won the ballot in November 1969, however, the results of the survey were still not known, and no date had been fixed for the publication of its findings.

In 1968 – 69 there had been a rash of private Members' Bills on the subject of the disabled. None of them had been successful. In July 1968 Jack Ashley, who had recently been stricken with total deafness, had returned to the House of Commons and had introduced under the Ten-Minute Rule a Disablement Income Commission Bill.[11] This procedure enabled him to make a short speech, in which he emphasized the need for specific financial help for disabled people. He received a unanimously sympathetic hearing, both for his courage in returning to the House under such a handicap and for the content of his speech. He was given leave to introduce the Bill but because it was so late in the session and because the Ten-Minute Rule procedure rarely leads to anything further, nothing more was done.

A renewed attempt was made by James Prior in December 1968. He had won fifth place in the ballot for private Members' Bills. His measure was called the Disabled Persons Pensions and Miscellaneous Provisions Bill, and had largely been drafted by the voluntary group Access for the Disabled. Any disabled people who did not qualify under the National Insurance scheme would have obtained a pension for the first time under the Bill, which also emphasized the needs of the disabled for adequate housing, access and related facilities. The Bill came up for Second Reading on February 21st 1969.[12] Although the general tenor of the debate was favourable, the Government had made it clear that it could not support the measure, mainly for financial reasons. As a result, a Second Reading was defeated on a division, by 112 votes to 76, and the Bill was lost.

Another Conservative backbencher, Gordon Campbell, had introduced a Bill to establish a Disablement Commission, an advisory body which would report to the Government on the financial needs of the disabled. This Bill too ran into Government opposition and was defeated on Second Reading, by 28 votes to 24, on March 28th 1969.[13] A similar Bill was introduced by Colonel Sir Tufton Beamish but was allowed to lapse in March 1970,[14] presumably because of the progress then being made by the Chronically Sick and Disabled Persons Bill.

In the year or two preceding Alf Morris's Bill, therefore, a number of unsuccessful backbench attempts had been made to legislate for the disabled. Their failure was in some senses discouraging, but they did at lease reveal a rising tide of interest and sympathy amongst Members of Parliament of all parties for the problems of the disabled.

When the ballot for private Members' Bills was held on November 6th 1969 Alf Morris was in India as a member of a Commonwealth Parliamentary Association delegation. He had not therefore been able to enter his name for the ballot himself, but had prudently arranged for his elder brother, Charles to put his name in for him. Alf Morris was unaware of his success in the ballot until two days later, when flying back from India to London, he read in a day-old *Guardian* that he had drawn first place.

Success in the ballot is a guarantee of an enormous postbag. There are many organizations, pressure groups and even individuals who prepare draft Bills in the hope that they will be able to persuade backbenchers who are successful in the ballot to legislate in their particular field. By the time Alf Morris arrived back to collect his mail, dozens of suggestions and many offers of already drafted Bills were waiting for him.

Over the next week or two more than 400 possibilities were mentioned to him. While most of these suggestions came from single-issue pressure groups, some of whom (like those concerned with changes in the law concerning abortion) exist solely to promote legislative change, many came from his parliamentary and ministerial colleagues. Indeed, as Alf Morris himself has remarked, the Government can be the most important pressure group of all. Every Government Department has a list of relatively minor legislation for which there is no parliamentary time available. If a backbench Member can be persuaded to take on some such piece of legislation, a Government Department can often secure some worthwhile legislative advance without eating into the time available for more important measures. For example, Alf Morris was asked by Arthur Skeffington, a junior Minister in the Ministry of Housing and Local Government, to introduce a small measure concerning the preservation of trees. Morris declined this suggestion but was able to help in placing this Bill with Duncan (now Lord) Sandys, then the MP for Streatham, who had won a lower place in the ballot; this Bill ultimately reached the Statute Book, having completed all its stages in the House of Lords[15] in less than half an hour, on the same day that Alf Morris's Bill also left the House of Lords.

Most MPs who win a high place in the ballot are happy to accept a Bill drafted for them by some external body or Government Department. Not only does this overcome the immediate problem of deciding on the scope of the measure and the terms in which it should be drafted, but it also guarantees the backbencher advice and assistance throughout the passage of the Bill. Most sponsors of private Members' Bills have ready-made secretarial help and expert advice made available to them by the body responsible for the original drafting of the Bill.

Despite these obvious advantages, Alf Morris decided to reject all the suggestions made to him and to use his opportunity to legislate in the field which he knew best. He accordingly chose to introduce the measure which eventually became the Chronically Sick and Disabled Persons Act, 1970. He was encouraged to do this by a small group of colleagues in local government, friends in voluntary organizations and Parliamentary colleagues who were fellow members of the All-Party Disablement Group; but the initial decision was his alone. He set about the task of drafting, without Government support or help from any outside agency, what was to become a major piece of legislation.

NOTES

1. *House of Lords Debates* (hereafter *H. L. Deb.*), vol. 310, col. 1117.
2. Arthur Butler and Alfred Morris, *No Feet to Drag*, Sidgwick & Jackson, London, 1972.
3. *House of Commons Debates (hereafter H. C. Deb.*), vol. 751, col. 1333.
4 *H. C. Deb.*, vol. 725, *col. 182; H. C. Deb.*, vol. 751, cols. 1333, 1334. *347;*
5. *H. C. Deb.*, vol. 751, cols. *350 – 1.*
6. *H. C. Deb.*, vol. 751, *col. 390.*
7. *H. C. Deb.*, vol. 722, *col. 90.*
8. *H. C. Deb.*, vol. 724, cols. 1788 – 91; *H. C. Deb.*, vol. 736, *cols. 800 – 3; H. C. Deb.*, vol. 774, *col. 304*
9. *Report of the Committee on Local Authority and Allied Personal Services* (the Seebohm Report), Cmnd 3703, HMSO, London, 1968. Paragraphs 316 – 36 deal with the needs of the physically handicapped, and paragraphs 337 – 72 with those of the mentally handicapped.
10. *H. C. Deb.*, vol. 751, col. 1332.
11. *H. C. Deb.*, vol. 768. col. 1256.
12. *H. C. Deb.*, vol. 778. cols. 943 – 1038
13. *H. C. Deb.*, vol. 780. cols. 1990 – 2034.
14. *H. C. Deb.*, vol. 798. col. 929.
15. *H. L. Deb.*, vol. 310, cols. 1144 – 1153; Trees Act 1970.

CHAPTER TWO

Policy and Procedure

It is a truism that the role of the backbencher in the modern Parliament is a declining one. It is Governments that dominate the legislative programme and the parliamentary timetable. It is Governments that make policy and control the executive. On those rare occasions when the Government cannot use its parliamentary majority to achieve its objectives, it is the rival front benches, through the 'usual channels', that reach agreement on what needs to be done. In all of this the ordinary backbencher is regarded as little more than lobby fodder, compelled to follow the party line despite the dictates of his own conscience or the interests of his constituents.

This picture, so unflattering to the backbencher, is not quite the whole truth, however. The narrow (or non-existent) parliamentary majorities of 1974 – 79 meant that backbenchers were able to exercise more power than is usually the case; it was, after all, through the efforts of backbenchers that the then Government's major legislation was wrecked, and it was a House of Commons defeat that brought down the Labour Government in 1979 and provoked a general election. But quite apart from the special parliamentary circumstances of that time, backbenchers have more power, or perhaps more influence, than is generally recognized. We have left behind the age of deference; the House of Commons now comprises many backbenchers of an independent turn of mind, and it is a foolish Leader of the House or Chief Whip who ignores backbench opinion. Backbenchers in today's Parliament are aware that determination and perseverance can make even an individual MP a force to be reckoned with by the Government, and that in the last resort it is they collectively who control Parliament, and therefore the Government, rather than the other way around.

Of course, it is only in extreme circumstances that backbenchers will foresake their own Government; that is in the nature of, and part of the strength of, party government. But Governments, and Oppositions as well, find that they can no longer rely on the blind obedience of backbenchers and on the unquestioned authority and disciplinary powers of their business managers. The process of government in Parliament is increasingly one of continuing negotiations between the party leaders and their own backbench supporters.

Differences in procedure reflect these changes in attitude. The major parties have evolved new methods for taking account of the growing backbench demand for a say in policy making. The Labour Party, for example, has worked hard (not, perhaps, altogether successfully) to involve backbenchers in subject groups which have some influence on policy making when the party is in power. Many backbench Labour MPs take part in the working parties set up while the Labour Party has been in Opposition to formulate new party policy. Parliament, too, has introduced changes to accommodate the demands of backbench Members of Parliament. Powerful new Select Committees have been established to monitor the activities of Government Departments, to advise Ministers and to hold Ministers accountable for their actions and policies.

But despite these changes, the Government remains the dominant element in the modern Parliament. Nowhere is this more true than in its virtual monopoly of the legislative programme and of the time available for legislation. Whereas in earlier centuries much legislation was introduced by individual Members of Parliament, usually by means of a petition supported by an MP's constituents, the overwhelming preponderance of modern legislation is drafted and introduced by the Government. The opportunities for the backbench Member to introduce legislation of his own are extremely limited.[1]

The major limitation is simply time. Only 20 days in each parliamentary session are set aside for private Members' business. Of those 20 days, only 10 or possibly 12 days (depending on a decision taken by the House in each session) are available for private Members' legislation; the remainder of the days available are devoted to private Members' motions. The amount of legislation that can be processed in a maximum of 12 days is obviously very small.

It is this lack of time rather than the procedural rules that works against the possibility of much private Members' legislation being carried through. In theory, a private Member has the same rights as a Minister as far as his right to introduce legislation is concerned. In both cases Standing Order No. 37 simply provides that a Member may, after notice, present a Bill without previously obtaining leave from the House. The difference lies solely in the fact that a Minister, introducing a Bill on behalf of the Government, will be secure in the knowledge that the Government will have made room in the timetable for the Bill to receive a Second Reading and to go on through its remaining stages. In the case of the private Member (unless he has made some arrangement with the Government) no such time will be available under this procedure, and in the absence of a formal, unopposed Second Reading (such absence being usually signified by an objection from one or more backbenchers) the Bill must fail.

Standing Order No. 37 is therefore used by backbenchers in two cases only. First, when it is clear that there is no prospect of proceeding with the legislation a backbencher may nevertheless feel it worthwhile to draft a Bill and to have it published in order to draw parliamentary, press and public attention to the subject of his Bill. A recent example was the Bill presented by Tony Benn and others to amend the European Communities Act.

The second case is when a private Member has reached agreement with the Government (and this may very often be on the Government's initiative) to introduce a small measure which will pass unopposed. Interestingly enough, Alf Morris himself was responsible for just such a Bill at the very same time as he was promoting the Chronically Sick and Disabled Persons Bill. By virtue of his former position as Parliamentary Private Secretary to the Minister of Agriculture, he had been approached by the Minister of Agriculture to see whether he would sponsor a small measure entitled the Food and Drugs (Milk) Bill. He had already agreed to do this when he won the ballot for private Members' Bills.

He proceeded with the agricultural measure which was presented for Second Reading[2] on the very same day (December 5th 1969) as the Chronically Sick and Disabled Persons Bill. The difference was that the Chronically Sick and Disabled Persons Bill was fully debated before being given a Second Reading, whereas the Food and Drugs (Milk) Bill, being non-controversial and having

Government support, was given an unopposed and formal Second Reading. The measure, whose purpose was to authorize the ultra-heat treatment of milk, subsequently passed through all its stages without ever having been debated by the House of Commons and eventually received the Royal Assent on January 19th 1970.[3] There are many examples of such small but nevertheless valuable measures which go on to the Statute Book through the agency of a backbench Member of Parliament. These instances cannot usually be regarded as true examples of backbench legislation, however, since the backbencher is in effect operating simply as an agent for the Government and is taking up virtually no parliamentary time.

There are occasions, however, when legislation introduced by a backbencher under Standing Order No. 37 does get on to the Statute Book and is genuinely private Members' legislation. This happened, for example, with Sidney Silverman's Bill to abolish the death penalty. He had introduced it as a piece of private initiative. The Government wished to support it but did not wish to be seen to be doing so officially. It therefore made room in the parliamentary timetable for the Bill to proceed, although the measure remained a piece of backbench legislation under the guidance of its sponsor.

A second method by which a backbencher might initiate legislation is under Standing Order No. 13. This is often referred to as the Ten-Minute Rule. Standing Order No. 13 provides that on Tuesdays and Wednesdays leave may be sought by private Members to introduce Bills. Notice should be given for a day no earlier than the fifth or later than the fifteenth sitting day after the day on which it is given; a Member may give notice in respect of no more than one Bill in any 15-day period. While one Member may give notice on behalf of another, the Public Bill Office may accept not more than one notice at a time from any one Member, and only one such application for leave shall be obtained in any one day.

Strictly speaking, the procedure under Standing Order No. 13 is not an essential provision. As we have already seen, Standing Order No. 37 offers backbenchers at all times the possibility of introducing a Bill without seeking leave from the House. The advantage of the Ten-Minute Rule procedure, however, is that the Speaker, at his discretion, may allow a brief explanatory statement (usually lasting about ten minutes) in support of the application and he may also allow a similarly brief speech if a Member wishes to oppose the Bill. If the Bill is opposed, a division may take place, but in either case the sponsor of the Bill has the advantage of being able to make a speech in its support.

It is for this reason that the procedure is very popular with backbench Members. The opportunity to seek leave to introduce a Bill, and therefore to make a ten-minute speech, arises at the commencement of public business, at the end of Question Time. This is a most favourable time, when the press galleries are still full and the Chamber relatively well-populated. The backbench Member is therefore able to attract a good deal of attention to the subject matter of his proposed Bill, and he may also obtain further marginal advantages. For example, if the matter is pressed to a division, a substantial number of Members will be present to vote, and he may well be able to discover, by studying the division list, whether the Government of the day favours or opposes his proposed measure and, more generally, from which directions support or opposition may be expected.

On the other hand, there are disadvantages in trying to use the Ten-Minute Rule procedure. Many speeches in support of an application are delivered amid the hubbub and distraction of a rapidly emptying Chamber as Members file out after Question Time, chatting among themselves and paying little attention to the vain attempts of a backbencher trying to promote his favourite cause. There are also occasions when the embarrassment takes a different form. A backbench Member who has innocently given notice a fortnight in advance that he wishes to apply for leave to introduce a Bill on a particular date may suddenly find himself speaking to a packed House of Commons, which has just been raised to a fever pitch by a particularly tendentious Prime Minister's Question Time or which is now impatient to move on to the opening speech of a crucial debate of major importance. In these circumstances the House is likely to deal harshly with the unfortunate backbenchers's efforts to interrupt business of prime national importance by referring to a matter which is regarded as being of very limited significance.

In any case, a Bill introduced under the Ten-Minute Rule suffers from the same disadvantage as a Bill introduced under Standing Order No. 37. In both cases progress is likely to be severely hampered unless the Government has agreed to provide time for further stages of the Bill. In most cases (for example, Jack Ashley's Disablement Income Commission Bill introduced in July 1968)[4] no further progress is made.

Many backbenchers who use this procedure have no intention or expectation of actually introducing legislation. They are concerned simply to obtain ten minutes of prime time in order to expound a favourite theme; they do not necessarily even bother to draft a Bill. This is increasingly regarded as an abuse of the House's procedure, and a Member who wishes to avail himself of the opportunity offered by the Ten-Minute Rule will generally be required to draft a Bill and to present it at the Public Bill Office.

The whole question of private Members' Bills introduced under Standing Order No. 37 or Standing Order No. 13, in circumstances in which there is no prospect of progress, is extremely puzzling to members of the public. There are many instances when outside bodies and individuals learn that a Bill is being introduced on a topic of interest to them and are mystified when the Bill seems to make no further progress. They are in most cases unaware that the Bill has been introduced simply as a publicity measure rather than as a serious attempt at legislation.

Sometimes, though, the Government is able to turn this confusion to its own advantage. An example of this was Sir Gerald Nabarro's Tobacco and Snuff (Health Hazards) Bill in 1970. Among other things, this required a health warning to be printed on cigarette packets. The Bill was not proceeded with, but the fact that the Government allowed it to receive an unopposed Second Reading increased the pressure on the tobacco companies to reach a voluntary agreement to print health warnings.

The best chance a private Member has of carrying legislation through to the Statute Book arises under Standing Order No. 6, which provides for a ballot for private Members' Bills. Bills introduced under this provision are then given priority on the days allocated in each session for private Members' Bills. (It was, of course, under this procedure that Alf Morris promoted the Chronically Sick and Disabled Persons Bill.) The ballot is held on the second Thursday of the session and is conducted by the Speaker. Those Members who are successful in the ballot must present a Bill of their choice at the commencement of public business on the fifth Wednesday of the Session. A day is then allocated for the Second Reading debate. Until this stage has been reached, a private Member may not avail himself of the opportunity provided by Standing Order No. 37 or Standing Order No. 13 to introduce any other Bill.

Since in practice twelve days are currently allocated in each session for private Members' legislation, and since half of those twelve days are devoted to Second Reading debates, it is usually the case that only the first six Members whose names are drawn in the ballot are likely to carry their Bill through into legislation. In Alf Morris's case, having come first in the ballot, he had a very real chance of actually placing a measure on the Statute Book.

Although someone who secures one of the top six places in the ballot can be sure of having time made available for the Second Reading debate, he will still have to secure a favourable vote. This becomes much less likely if it is known that the Government opposes his measure. Many Members of the Government party will find it prudent to take the Government line and a backbench Member may find that he is unable to construct a majority for his Bill. So, even under this procedure, the Government's attitude may be crucial.

There is also the problem that private Members' Bills are debated on Fridays. This is the day when most Members of Parliament, particularly those from far-flung constituencies, like to get away in order to undertake constituency engagements, hold their advice surgeries and perhaps even see their families. They will stay behind to vote on a private Member's Bill only if they feel particularly strongly about it and if they can be assured that their presence and vote will be necessary.

This means that even if a backbench sponsor manages to avoid Government opposition, he may still be vulnerable to the opposition of more or less organized groups from anywhere in the House. The opponents of his Bill may decide that they will 'talk it out' — that is, they will attempt to continue the debate beyond 2.30 p.m.,[5] when business normally ends and when a vote would normally be taken. If this looks likely to happen, the sponsor of the Bill must apply the Closure, but for this he must obtain the Speaker's permission. If permission is granted, he must still secure a majority if the application for a Closure is opposed. Not only must he obtain a majority of those present, but the number of those present, as revealed by those voting in such a division, must total 100 or more. The opponents may therefore simply refuse to go into the Division Lobby, apart from providing tellers, and will therefore impose upon the sponsor of the Bill the obligation to retain 100 supporters in order to obtain the Closure. There are several instances of Bills failing when majorities in favour of the Closure have been obtained but fewer than 100 members have been present. Even where no opposition to the Closure is mounted, the sponsor of the Bill must maintain a 'House' of 40 Members in case a division should be called on Second Reading. It is not always easy to persuade one's colleagues to be present at 2.30 p.m. on a Friday afternoon, particularly when it is not clear whether their presence will be required on not.

The stage following the Second Reading, as with all public legislation, is the Committee stage. The major difference between the Committee stage of a private Member's Bill and that of other public legislation is that in the latter case the Committee will comprise a majority of Government supporters, whereas in the case of a private Member's Bill, the Committee will normally comprise a majority of those favourable to the Bill, irrespective of party affiliations. Support for and interest in a Bill is usually, but not exclusively, evidenced by speeches made in the Second Reading debate.

This built-in majority does not guarantee success, however. Opponents of a Bill may still be able to kill it by tabling a large number of amendments, and speaking at length on each of them, so that the Bill cannot take its place in the queue for the few private Member's days which are available and does not therefore complete its remaining stages. The backbench sponsor of a private Member's Bill is under two major disadvantages by comparison with the promoters of a Government Bill in trying to deal with these tactics. First, he is unable to obtain any timetable or guillotine motion and therefore has no defence against filibustering tactics. Second, he does not have the services of a whip to try to persuade or organize his supporters to vote in concert, nor does he have the powers of patronage which are available to the Government and which are extremely helpful in keeping potentially recalcitrant supporters in line.

These problems are also apparent when it comes to other aspects of the Committee stage. Valuable time may be lost if a quorum is not maintained; the maintenance of a quorum is usually the responsibility of the Government whip but the private Member who is sponsoring his own Bill will find that, among all his other responsibilities, he also has the duty of making sure that his supporters actually remain in the Committee Room.

Nevertheless, the Committee stage of a private Member's Bill has some features which represent an improvement over the Committee stage of a Government Bill. The Committee Stage is usually one of the least satisfactory aspects of parliamentary procedure. As we have seen, the Committee for an ordinary piece of Government legislation is drawn up along strictly party lines so that the Government always has a majority. The result is that whatever the content of the debate, the Government will expect to use its majority to win any division that may be called. While debates and votes along party lines may be suitable for determining the broad outlines of a piece of legislation, they are not necessarily the best means of dealing with the detailed amendments to the provisions of a Bill. Whereas the supposed purpose of the Committee stage is to give detailed consideration to the Bill so that it is accurately drafted to secure its objectives, this purpose may often be obscured by the battle fought out by the front benches of the two main Parties, who may have rather different aims in mind.

The Government front bench is concerned simply to get the Bill through the Committee with as few changes as possible. To this end, Government backbench members of the Committee are enjoined to say nothing, but to vote when required. As a result, service on the Standing Committee of a Government Bill is usually a complete waste of time for a Government backbencher. The Opposition front bench, on the other hand, may well wish to use the time available to it in order to emasculate the Bill or to extract some important concession from the Government. In this respect, its only weapon is delay, since it can be out-voted on any issue by the Government's in-built majority on the Committee. As a consequence, Opposition backbenchers are encouraged to speak at inordinate length in the early stages of the Committee in order to put pressure on the Government's timetable. Since Government backbenchers say nothing, the debate is one-sided, repetitive and boring, and usually only just manages to stay within the rules of order as to relevance.

The Government may respond to these tactics by making concessions to the Opposition in return for an informally agreed timetable; alternatively, it may decide to take the hard way by testing the stamina of the Opposition through a series of all-night sittings. In either case, proper scrutiny of the Bill becomes a secondary consideration. Many Committee stages are disfigured by an attempt at filibustering by the Opposition, followed either by Government concessions or Opposition acknowledgement of defeat and a rapid canter through the remaining provisions of the Bill.

The Committee stage of a private Member's Bill usually manages to avoid many of these problems. Party lines are, of course, much less strictly drawn; and, while a majority which is in favour of the Bill is usually assured on the Committee, opinions may well vary on the merits of each individual issue arising on successive amendments and clauses. Although the Government usually has a Minister on the Committee to put the Government viewpoint, it is not usual for the Opposition to be represented by an official front bench spokesman, and the usual clash of party positions is thereby avoided. Available time is regulated less by the party battle and more by the intrinsic importance of the provisions being considered. The Committee is inclined to reach conclusions on the basis of the arguments produced, rather than on the voting strength of the various factions. The Chronically Sick and Disabled Persons Bill demonstrated many of these advantages. It was remarkable in its Committee stage for not having a single division and for the spirit of conciliation and constructive purpose which marked its proceedings.

The Committee stage is not, however, the end of the obstacle race. Even if it is successfully negotiated, the private Member's Bill will have to compete with others for the limited time available. Again, the Government's attitude is crucial. If the Bill has suffered even a minimal delay in returning to the floor of the House for the Report stage, an unsympathetic Government can kill it by refusing to make more time available. On the other hand, well-disposed business managers may, exceptionally, make extra time available for Bills upon which they look kindly. This was particularly evident in the term of the Labour Government from 1964 to 1970, and Alf Morris's Bill was eventually a beneficiary of this kind of Government support. The extra time may be made available through the provision of additional sittings or through sittings extended beyond 10 o'clock at night.

Once the Bill has completed its passage through the House of Commons, it must then face the hurdle of the House of Lords. In most cases, the House of Lords will not set out to destroy or frustrate a private Member's Bill which has been approved by the

House of Commons. In the case of the Chronically Sick and Disabled Persons Bill, however, the hazard was of a different nature; an enthusiastic body of supporters in the House of Lords very nearly killed the Bill by trying to cram more into it than was possible in the time available.

One of the major limitations on the ability of the private Member to introduce legislation is the rule that only the Government can bring in a Bill which imposes a charge on the national revenues. This means that a private Member must either choose a Bill which involves no such charge, or he must obtain from the Government a Financial Resolution which will cover the expenditure involved. This second course, which was that eventually and successfully pursued by Alf Morris, again means that the private Member is entirely dependent on Government support for his measure. While this may seem to place the private Member at an unfair disadvantage, the rationale of the rule is to be supported; otherwise private Members could introduce measures, in an attempt to secure an electoral advantage, which required the expenditure of large sums of public money on causes of particular benefit to their constituents.

Despite all these obstacles, a good deal of private Members' legislation survives the course and has been of particular value, expecially in the field of social reform. Over recent years private Members' legislation has secured reforms in the fields of homosexuality, abortion, contraception, divorce, the abolition of theatre censorship, the rehabilitation of offenders, the conservation of wild creatures, the law governing mobile homes, industrial common ownership, consumer safety and many others.

The fact remains, however, that the one issue which is most important in determining the success or failure of private Members' legislation is the question of whether or not the Government can be induced to support a measure, or at the very least to remain neutral. A Government which is determined to kill a backbench measure will almost always succeed.

NOTES

1. See generally on this topic, Peter G. Richards, *The Backbenchers,* 2nd edn., Faber, London, 1974.

2. *H. C. Deb.*, vol. 792, col. 1940.
3. *H. C. Deb.*, vol. 794, col. 1800.
4. *See p. 5.*
5. *Until the 1979 – 80 session Friday sittings were from 11 a.m. to 4 p.m. In 1979, however, the hours were changed so that the House now sits on Fridays from 9.30 a.m. to 2.30 p.m.*

CHAPTER THREE

The Drafting and Presentation of the Bill

As we have seen,[1] Standing Orders provide that the ballot for private Members' Bills is to be held on the second Thursday of the session and that the Bills so balloted will be presented by those successful in the ballot at the commencement of public business on the fifth Wednesday of the Session. In 1969 the ballot was held on November 6th; but because Alf Morris was in India at the time, he did not hear of his success until November 8th. This meant that he had to decide on the subject matter for his Bill and present it for First Reading within 18 days, that is, on November 26th.

Apart from the decision as to what the Bill should be about, this first stage of the timetable in itself presented no great problem. The First Reading of a Bill does not require that it should be presented in full draft form; all that is required is a 'dummy' Bill with a title. On the other hand, if Alf Morris were to take his place in the Parliamentary timetable, head the queue for Second Readings, get his Bill into Committee as quickly as possible and so maximize his chances of completing all its stages before the end of the session, he had to have a Bill fully drafted for Second Reading as quickly as possible. The first day for Second Reading of private Members' Bills was December 5th; if Alf Morris were not ready for this date, he would slip down the queue and jeopardize his chances of getting his Bill through. It is also the convention that the House should not be presented with the Second Reading of the Bill without having had adequate time to consider its contents. This meant that a draft Bill, fully printed and available to Members must be produced at least a week before Second Reading – in this case, by November 28th. It was this deadline that Alf Morris had to meet.

Among the 400 or more suggestions made to Alf Morris, there were those which would have allowed him to take a ready-made Bill 'off the shelf' and which would therefore have enabled him to meet the tight deadline with relative ease. However, Alf Morris decided almost immediately that he would try to legislate in his particular field of interest; the difficulty here was that none of the voluntary organizations had thought in terms of legislation, and no ready-made Bill was available. It was this need to draft the Bill from scratch that imposed a considerable strain on the sponsor of the Chronically Sick and Disabled Persons Bill, both from the viewpoint of meeting the deadline for publication of the Bill and throughout its remaining stages.

As soon as Alf Morris announced that he intended to legislate on provision for the disabled, he was offered a number of suggestions from interested organizations and bodies for what should be included in the Bill. As he himself has described, he set about drawing up a catalogue of such suggestions and drafting them in the form that they would take if they were the subject of Early Day Motions. (Most backbenchers have some experience of drafting Early Day Motions, which are simply expressions of opinion printed on the Order Paper in the names of their sponsors and those of other sympathetic backbench MPs in the hope that these opinions will influence the Government. While they must be drafted with sufficient care to express accurately the sentiments of the signatories, they are in no sense intended to be legislative provisions, and they therefore give little practical guidance to an inexperienced backbencher who is suddenly confronted with the task of drafting a major Bill.)

Although Alf Morris subsequently obtained the help and advice of Parliamentary Counsel and of the legal officers of the various Government Departments concerned, he began the task of drafting his Bill without expert advice from anyone. It is little wonder that the Bill as originally drafted was seriously defective and that this in turn caused a series of problems throughout its remaining stages. Alf Morris was aware of these problems, however, and constantly reminded his supporters that the Bill would need continual redrafting and polishing as it proceeded.

One of the first people to whom he turned for advice about what should be in the Bill was the then Chief Welfare Officer of the City of Manchester, Mr Clifford Hilditch. As a Manchester Member of Parliament, Alf Morris had naturally built up a close professional relationship with Mr Hilditch, and they had a common interest in the problems of the disabled. Mr Hilditch offered a number of suggestions and provided advice throughout the passage of the Bill through Parliament. Another Chief Welfare Officer, Mr J. Gardham, of Kingston-upon-Hull, also got in touch with Alf Morris to make a number of suggestions about the contents of the Bill. At this preliminary stage Alf Morris made contact with a number of voluntary organizations in the field, and he held talks particularly with Mr Marsh Dickson of the National Campaign for the Young Chronic Sick, with the Disablement Income Group and with the Central Council for the Disabled. Some of his closest advisers were those of his Parliamentary colleagues who were members of the All-Party Disablement Group at Westminster. The Secretary of this group was John Astor, who had strong links with the Disablement Income Group; other leading contributors to discussions at this point were Neil Marten and Alf Morris's three Labour colleagues, Jack Ashley (the chairman of the All-Party Disablement Group), Laurie Pavitt and Lewis Carter-Jones.

Many of the provisions of the original Bill, published in the nick of time on November 26th, owed their origins to suggestions from this group. In the Bill as originally published, for example, Clause 31, providing for special educational treatment for the deaf-blind, was the suggestion of Jack Ashley; Clause 22, aimed at the prevention of discrimination against deaf people in employment, originated with Laurie Pavitt, as did Clauses 23 and 24 on the training of the deaf and the setting up of an Institute for Hearing Research. Other Members made special contributions on particular provisions. Syd Bidwell, for example, had earlier introduced under the Ten-Minute Rule a Bill to extend the provision of chiropody services, and he was particularly interested in Clause 16. One of the provisions whose origin can be traced most directly to a particular Member of Parliament is Clause 26 of the original Bill, which provided for an annual report to be made by the Minister of Technology each year on the research and development programmes undertaken for the benefit of disabled persons. This Clause originated in a chance meeting between Alf Morris and Tony Benn, then Minister of Technology. The two had met in the Tea Room and had fallen into conversation about Alf Morris's forthcoming Bill. Tony Benn had put the suggestion that his Ministry should produce an annual report and, with Alf Morris, quickly composed a rough draft of the provision on the back of an envelope. On the following day Alf Morris had a telephone call from Tony Benn's Private Secretary, which confirmed that the Minister intended to proceed with his suggestion, and a number of drafting suggestions to improve the Clause were made. This Clause was substantially modified in later proceedings but eventually passed into law.

The provenance of other Clauses can also be traced to the interest and suggestions of outside bodies and individuals. Clause 25, on the use of invalid carriages on highways, was the brainchild of Lady Hoare, founder of the Thalidomide Trust, and resulted from her work with Thalidomide children. Access for the Disabled was responsible for the suggestion, which originally appeared as Clause 5, on access to toilet facilities for the disabled. Clause 7, providing for information about disabled children to be transmitted from educational authorities to social services departments, was suggested by the Manchester and Salford Cripples' Help Society, while Lady Hamilton of the Disabled Living Foundation suggested both Clause 12 on housing advisory committees and Clause 21 on the training of persons working with disabled people. One of the most important provisions in the Bill, which originally appeared as Clause 20 and concerned the admission of young people to geriatric wards, was brought to Alf Morris's attention by Mr Marsh Dickson of the National Campaign for the Young Chronic Sick and by Miss Pamela La Fane, who had herself had the experience of being a young disabled person in a geriatric ward.

A number of MPs, through their connections with voluntary groups, were able to make suggestions. Neil Marten, for example, through his interest in the Disabled Drivers' Association, was particularly concerned with the question of mobility for disabled people. At a later stage John Golding, a member of the Post Office Engineering Union, helped with the provision to provide telephone services to the disabled. The provision, which eventually became Section 14 on the inclusion of disabled people on consumers' consultative councils, was drafted by Fred Evans.

One group of people whose co-operation was clearly important to the prospects of the Bill was Government Ministers. One of the difficulties which Alf Morris encountered throughout the passage of the Bill was the fact that his Bill affected a large number of Government Departments; indeed, when provisions of the Bill were finally extended to Scotland and Northern Ireland a total of no fewer than eleven or twelve Government Departments was involved. The Department most directly affected was, of course, the Department of Health and Social Security (DHSS). At an early stage, before he had begun to draft his Bill, Alf Morris arranged to meet Richard Crossman, then Secretary of State, in order to advise him of his plans and to try to obtain his co-operation.

Alf Morris recalls that he met Richard Crossman in his ministerial room in the House of Commons at about 9.30 p.m., just before a 10 o'clock division. His reception was unhelpful. Crossman's initial reaction was that if legislation were needed in this field, his own Department would have introduced it. (This reaction is perhaps not uncommon when a departmental Minister is threatened with a private Member's Bill which seems to encroach on his territory.) Crossman was also very preoccupied with a massive piece of legislation which his Department was about to introduce under his guidance. The National Superannuation and Social Insurance Bill was to be a fundamental reorganization of pensions and would be the crowning achievement of Crossman's tenure of office at the Department. It was already clear that a piece of legislation of such massive proportions would have difficulty in getting through all its stages in the time available. Dick Crossman was clearly unwilling that any departmental or parliamentary attention should be diverted to a Bill which, as he saw it, was of only limited importance.

Presumably as a result of these considerations, Crossman not only refused to offer any co-operation but made it clear that he would try to frustrate Alf Morris at every point. The only constructive suggestion he made was that the Department had already drafted a minor provision to amend the Human Tissues Act so as to provide for an easier procedure to facilitate organ transplants. Crossman suggested that full departmental co-operation would be available to Alf Morris if he were prepared to take on this Bill instead of his own proposed measure. Morris pointed out that a non-controversial measure of this type could easily be introduced under Standing Order No. 37 and with Government support, could expect a speedy passage through the House. He felt that to use his first place in the ballot for such a measure would be to waste the opportunity provided to legislate more significantly.

When Alf Morris emerged, somewhat shaken, from his unhelpful meeting with Crossman, he reported the proceedings to his close colleagues Lewis Carter-Jones and Jack Ashley, who were also vitally interested in the success of Morris's initiative. Lewis Carter-Jones recalls that he saw Crossman immediately afterwards in the division lobby and that a spirited exchange took place between them.

Alf Morris completes the account of his relations with Crossman over the Bill by recalling that towards the end of January he ran into Richard Crossman in the House of Commons Tea Room. Crossman appeared to have no recollection of their earlier exchange and commented that he was delighted that the Chronically Sick and Disabled Persons Bill was making such good progress; by this time, of course, the Department, and particularly Dr John Dunwoody, who represented the Department in the Committee stage, had moved to a position of cautious endorsement of the objects of the Bill. Tam Dalyell, Richard Crossman's Parliamentary Private Secretary at the time, confirms[2] that Crossman tried to bully Alf Morris into changing the Bill drastically or dropping it altogether and also expressed the opinion that the DHSS would not itself have produced any similar legislation. Perhaps significantly, Richard Crossman makes no mention at all of the Alf Morris Bill in his Diaries.

Alf Morris's relations with other Government Departments were a little less chequered. He received a good deal of co-operation from the outset from the Ministry of Housing and Local Government and particularly from Reg Freeson, the junior Minister for Housing. Tony Benn's co-operative attitude at the Ministry of Technology has already been mentioned, and Morris was similarly encouraged by John Silkin at the Department of Public Building and Works. The response from the Treasury, on the other hand, was distinctly cool, and no positive help was offered; Alf Morris was told that the question of a Money Resolution 'would be considered'.

Co-operation of a particularly valuable nature was offered to Alf Morris by Mr Giles Ecclestone of the Public Bill Office in the House of Commons. Reference has already been made to the difficulties facing an inexperienced backbencher in drafting a Bill from scratch; staff of the House of Commons working in the Public Bill Office are not themselves parliamentary draftsmen, but they do have a good basic knowledge of the rules of procedure and of the form which legislation should take. Mr Giles Ecclestone, who acted as Clerk to the Standing Committee, was able to give Alf Morris a great deal of useful advice, which undoubtedly saved time and trouble at later stages. David Weitzman QC, who became a member of the Standing Committee, was also able to draw on his experience to offer legal and drafting advice.

The Bill as originally published on November 26th looked very different from the Bill which eventually reached the Statute Book. Many of the original provisions were withdrawn or rejected at later stages; every provision which did survive was modified, some quite substantially; and new Clauses were added to the Bill as it proceeded. Of the 31 substantive Clauses in the Bill as originally published, no fewer than 10 had disappeared entirely by the time the Bill had reached the Statute Book. These included Clause 7, imposing on education authorities the duty to inform social work departments of disabled children within their areas; Clause 8, providing that the special needs of the disabled should be included in any assessment of needs undertaken by local authorities; Clause 9, providing travel concessions for those suffering from severe visual defects, short of total blindness; Clause 11, setting up an advisory council to administer an attendance allowance; Clause 17, extending the provision of four-wheeled vehicles; Clause 18, providing vehicles to persons too disabled to drive; Clause 22, forbidding employers to discriminate against the deaf; Clause 23, providing for the training of the deaf; Clause 27, relaxing the rules relating to the service disability pension; and Clause 30, amending the earnings rule for the wives of men drawing sickness benefit.

The final Act, on the other hand, contained a number of new Clauses which were not present in the original Bill. These included, most importantly, Section 28, enabling the Secretary of State to define some of the key expressions in the Act; Sections 14 and 15, providing for the presence on consumers' consultative committees and local authorities committees of people with experience of working with the disabled; Section 21, providing for the Orange Badge Scheme of parking concessions for disabled drivers and the drivers of disabled passengers; Section 23, regulating the war pensions appeals procedure; and Sections 26 and 27, providing special educational treatment for autistic and dyslexic children.

Despite these major changes to the Bill between its first

appearance and its eventual enactment, the original Bill nevertheless contained much of importance which survived into the final stage. These Clauses, which were almost all renumbered as they were amended or replaced, included provisions for the gathering of information about the number of disabled and the provision of information about the services available; special provision of services for the disabled, including telephone equipment and radio and television licences; provision for the special housing needs of the disabled, access to public buildings and the availability of appropriate toilet facilities (these provisions were much extended); regular meetings for the chairmen of war pensions committees; the requirement that advisory committees on housing, national insurance, industrial injuries and youth employment should include people with experience of working with the disabled; courses for medical practitioners on the technical equipment needed for the disabled; the admission of young people to geriatric wards; training courses for those concerned with the employment of the disabled; the establishment of an Institute of Hearing Research; and special education for the deaf-blind.

Some Clauses had a particularly chequered history. Section 19, for example, concerning the provision of chiropody services, began life as Clause 16 but was in much harder form; the Clause was not moved in Committee and disappeared for a time but eventually returned in the House of Lords Committee stage in its new form.

The Second Reading debate, based on the Bill as published on November 26th, took place on December 5th 1969.[3] In the first minute or two of his introductory speech[4], Alf Morris referred to the fact that he had had less than three weeks in which to prepare the Bill and that it was a 'collective essay', to which Members on both sides of the House and countless organizations and individuals outside had contributed. He realised that there 'may be imperfections of phrasing in parts of the essay which will require careful study ... and which may not entirely please, nor even survive, the assessors in Standing Committee'.

He began by thanking his brother Charles for having entered his name in the private Members' ballot. He was still clearly very uncertain about the sort of welcome he could expect for the Bill from the Government and had identified in his own mind the shortage of financial resources as being the most likely obstacle which would be placed in his way. He therefore devoted a substantial time in the early part of his speech to the point that many of his proposals, while certainly costing money, might also save it by allowing disabled people to work in the community and by enabling them to make a proper contribution.

He then stressed the importance of drawing up a register of disabled people so that the welfare of such people could be improved. It was at this point, relatively early in his speech, that he was interrupted[5] by John M. Temple, Conservative MP for the City of Chester and Vice-President of the Association of Municipal Authorities, who inquired about the definition of disabled people, a point which was to cause concern right through to the very latest stages of the Bill's passage. Alf Morris replied that he was conscious of the need for further definition and that he hoped that more detailed consideration could be given to this point in Standing Committee.

He then referred to a number of people who had suggested various provisions of the Bill. He cited, for example, the case of Mr Marsh Dickson, President of the National Campaign for the Young Chronic Sick. He also paid tribute to his own city of Manchester, as providing a good example of concern for the disabled, and to the Co-operative Party, which had always expressed an interest in the problems of the disabled. (One constituency case which he referred to, and which was the stimulus for Clause 9 of the Bill, concerned a semi-blind girl who received no help in getting to and from school. It subsequently emerged in Committee that existing regulations should have covered this case, and the Clause did not therefore survive into the later stages.) Alf Morris referred to the contributions made by colleagues such as Neil Marten, Fred Evans and Lewis Carter-Jones on issues like driving for the disabled, and Laurie Pavitt and Jack Ashley on help for the deaf. He concluded with a detailed explanation of the provisions of Clause 25, relating to the use of invalid carriages on footpaths. As it later turned out, this was the one Clause in the original Bill which survived relatively unscathed in the final Act, and the fact that Alf Morris spent some time in explaining it at Second Reading suggests that he had more confidence (justifiably, as it happened) that this Clause was properly drafted than he had in any other provisions of the Bill.

The debate began at 11.05 on the Friday morning and continued through the afternoon. Most of those who were later to take an active part in supporting the Bill, through becoming members of the Standing Committee, spoke in support of the Bill. One such supporter, Neil Marten, referred early in his speech to the difficulties of the person who draws the top place in the ballot and who accordingly has the shortest time in which to prepare it. 'I know', he said, 'that the Hon. Member has been under great pressure. It would be rather nice if we could give thought to this matter so that a little more time might be allowed for the preparation of the Bill which, I hope, will find its way on to the Statute Book.'[6]

The Second Reading debate is wide-ranging and may cover the whole ground of the Bill; indeed it may sometimes cover more than the precise provisions of the Bill itself, provided that speeches are made within the general area with which the Bill is dealing. In the debate on the Chronically Sick and Disabled Persons Bill most speakers made relatively short contributions, mindful of the Speaker's appeal to the effect that short speeches would enable more Members to speak in the debate. Accordingly, most of the speeches singled out one or two aspects of the Bill for consideration. Jack Ashley, for example, spoke of the particular problems of the deaf-blind. He did, however, describe the Bill as a 'charter for the chronic sick and disabled',[7] and this expression was used by subsequent speakers in succeeding stages of the Bill. Another early speaker in the debate was John Astor, the Secretary of the All-Party Disablement Group; he referred particularly to the contribution which was being made by the Disablement Income Group in drawing attention to the problems of the disabled. He expressed some reservations about the principle of providing special concessions for any one group of people and also agreed that the problem of defining the chronically sick and severely disabled had not yet been solved.

Jim Prior, though not speaking from the Conservative Front Bench on this occasion, congratulated Alf Morris on 'making certain that the Leader of the House was here to listen to his speech and, I presume, as well to give this Bill a fair passage through the House because it should, perhaps with some modification, be put on the Statute Book'.[8] The Leader of the House was Fred Peart, Alf Morris's friend and colleague, who was principally responsible for arranging the Government's parliamentary timetable and who was to play a considerable part in ensuring Government support for the measure. Jim Prior also referred to the Government's social survey of the extent of disablement in Britain and wondered how long the House would have to wait for the results. He singled out Clause 30, dealing with the earnings rule, as perhaps the most important provision in the Bill (the Clause was one of those which did not survive).

Paul Dean, speaking for the Opposition from the Dispatch Box, joined in the congratulations to Alf Morris and said that there was no Bill he would like to see promoted more than this one. He welcomed the Bill in principle and also expressed some support for the idea of a register of the disabled. He mentioned the problem of co-ordinating the activities of as many as 'seven different Departments' which might be involved in dealing with the disabled.

This speech was followed immediately by that of Dr John Dunwoody, the Joint Under-Secretary of State at the DHSS, speaking for the Government. He began by welcoming 'any opportunity in dealing with the problems of the chronic sick and disabled' and thanked Alf Morris for 'providing us with such a first-class opportunity'. He added, 'I am deeply impressed with the way in which he has brought a complicated Private Member's Bill before the House.'[9] He hoped that the House would give the Bill a Second Reading but warned that it was a complex and intricate subject, and that it might turn out that some of the provisions duplicated powers which already existed. He referred to the Government's intention to introduce legislation on the basis of the Seebohm Report and to the forthcoming Green Paper on the reorganization of the National Health Service. Another important consideration, he maintained, was the impending introduction of the National Superannuation Bill, and he forecast that the results of the Government's social survey would not be available until the middle of the following year.

Mr A. H. McDonald referred to the problem that the Bill appeared to impose a number of duties whose execution would require the expenditure of money, but made no reference to financial provision (apart from Clause 32, in italics, which could not be considered until a Money Resolution had been approved). He understood why this was so, he said (he was referring to the rule that public expenditure can only be agreed to on the recommendation of the Crown) but still expressed concern at the imposition of mandatory duties on local authorities.

Apart from Alf Morris himself, no fewer than 20 speakers, including the two frontbench spokesmen, took part in the debate. The debate ended at 3.30 p.m., and the Bill was given an unopposed Second Reading. The first major hurdle had been cleared, and the unanimous welcome given to the Bill was an encouraging sign; but the real difficulties were just beginning.

NOTES

1. See p. 14.
2. In a letter to Alf Morris dated 25 August 1977.
3. *H. C. Deb.*, vol. 792, cols. 1851 – 1934.
4. *H. C. Deb.*, vol. 792, cols. 1851 – 63.
5. *H. C. Deb.*, vol. 792, col. 1854.
6. *H. C. Deb.*, vol. 792, col. 1864.
7. *H. C. Deb.*, vol. 792, col. 1869.
8. *H. C. Deb.*, vol. 792, col. 1888.
9. *H. C. Deb.*, vol. 792, col. 1912.

CHAPTER FOUR

The Passage of the Bill through both Houses of Parliament

The Committee Stage

The procedure for a private Member's Bill is exactly the same as for Government legislation. In each case the Bill is referred to a Standing Committee for detailed consideration, following a decision by the House as a whole to give it a Second Reading. The Standing Committee then reports back to the House, which considers the changes that the Committee has made. The Bill is then given a Third Reading, in most cases a formality. The whole procedure is then repeated in the House of Lords. The Bill finally returns to the Commons, which accepts or rejects the changes made by the Lords.

Following its Second Reading, the Chronically Sick and Disabled Persons Bill was referred to Standing Committee C. Although the Committee is described as a Standing Committee, it is in fact *ad hoc* in its membership, and the Committee for Alf Morris's Bill was drawn up to include many of those who had expressed interest in the Bill, either in the preliminary drafting or in the Second Reading debate.

The committee comprised sixteen members, including two Government Ministers. It is customary for the Government to be represented by a Minister, even in a Standing Committee on a private Member's Bill, and on this occasion the scope of the Bill was felt to require the presence of two Ministers – Reg Freeson, Joint Parliamentary Secretary of the Ministry of Housing and Local Government, and Dr John Dunwoody, Joint Under-Secretary of State at the DHSS. Even so, these two Ministers found that the Bill raised issues which took them beyond the normal confines of their Departments. On occasions, the two Ministers were obliged to consult very widely with ministerial colleagues throughout Whitehall, and found that they were often speaking on behalf of other Government Departments. (This is extremely unusual, given the jealousy in Whitehall with which departmental responsibilities are guarded, and was yet another way in which the Chronically Sick and Disabled Persons Bill broke new ground.)

As far as the backbench Members were concerned, the Committee's composition reflected the principle that a Committee normally represents the range of opinion in the House as a whole at the time of Second Reading. Since all speeches at Second Reading had been in favour of the Bill, and it had been given an unopposed Second Reading, the Committee not unnaturally comprised supporters of its provisions. Almost all the backbench Members had spoken at Second Reading: Jack Ashley, John Astor, Sir Clive Bossom, Lewis Carter-Jones, Fred Evans, John Golding, Neil Marten, John Page, Laurie Pavitt and Jim Prior had all made speeches at this stage. Maurice Macmillan, who had had a longstanding interest in the disabled, Dame Irene Ward and David Weitzman were also added to the Committee.

It is not customary, on a private Member's Bill Committee, for the Opposition to be represented officially by a frontbench spokesman. This was also true of Standing Committee C and, as a result, although the Government's official position was made clear by the two Ministers on the Committee, no official spokesman for the Opposition was present. Alf Morris did, however, remain in touch, throughout the Committee stage and beyond, with Opposition spokesmen, whose views became increasingly important as the date of the general election grew nearer. He was assured throughout of Opposition support for his Bill.

The Committee was under the chairmanship of Sir Myer Galpern. His position was crucial; he was in charge of the procedure to be followed in the Committee and could therefore provide considerable help to Alf Morris, whose inexperience made the task of piloting the Bill through the Committee a particularly onerous one. This co-operation was particularly evident in Sir Myer's willingness to accept procedure motions at the beginning of each sitting, so that Alf Morris could deal with the provisions of the Bill in the order which he preferred.

The Committee Clerks to the Bill were Mr Giles Ecclestone and Miss J. Beeston. Mr Ecclestone, from the Public Bill Office, had already been involved with Alf Morris in the drafting of the Bill and again was able to keep a sympathetic eye on proceedings from his position at the Chairman's left hand.

The first sitting of the Committee was held on Wednesday December 17th at the usual hour of 10.30 a.m. The Bill had to go into Committee only twelve days after Second Reading, so that again Alf Morris had had very little time in which to take account of the points made at Second Reading and, more particularly, of the points which had flooded in from interested bodies and individuals outside Parliament. He was compelled to go for an early Committee day, however, because his Bill would otherwise have fallen behind in the queue, and another Bill, perhaps already drafted to perfection, would have been ready to step into its place.

Representations and queries

Between Second Reading and the Christmas recess no fewer than 26 voluntary organizations for the handicapped wrote to Alf Morris with comments on the Bill. These included a number of organizations, such as the National Society for Autistic Children, whose suggestions eventually found their way into the Bill. In addition a large number of individuals wrote in; these included the Chief Welfare Officers of a number of local authorities, including Bromley and Kingston-upon-Hull, as well as the Chief Welfare Officer of Alf Morris's own city of Manchester. Another important contributor was Alderman H. Davis of Lancashire County Council, a Labour councillor of many years' experience of working with the disabled. A number of medical experts also wrote to Alf Morris. These included Dr Peter Taylor of the London School of Hygiene and Tropical Medicine, Dr P. J. R. Nicholls of the Nuffield Orthopaedic Centre and Professor Margot Jefferys of Bedford College. Contributions were also received from the associations of local authorities.

The Association of Municipal Corporations was particularly concerned, as were a number of other contributors, about the problem of definition. They asked whether the category covered by Alf Morris's Bill was the same category as that defined in Section

29 of the National Assistance Act 1948. The London School of Hygiene and Tropical Medicine suggested, on the other hand, that the definition used in the Disabled Persons (Employment) Act 1944, might be used; this was thought, however, to cover too many people and to include many who, though disabled, were not substantially impaired in their mobility.

One of the ways in which the problem of definition frustrated a possible object of the Act was demonstrated when Alf Morris raised with the Treasury the question of a special income tax allowance for the disabled, similar to the allowance given to the blind. The Treasury's negative reply was based on the difficulty of arriving at a workable definition of disablement. It also made the general point that financial help for the disabled should come directly through social security, and not indirectly through the tax system.

A number of Chief Welfare Officers and other local authority members were concerned that the Bill, as originally drafted, imposed duties on local health authorities as opposed to social services departments. The confusion over this point perhaps reflected the uncertainty preceding the implementation of the Seebohm Report on the reorganization of social services departments.

A number of people emphasized the importance of the registration of disabled people. Mr Gardham, Chief Welfare Officer of Hull, made the point that registration should be a voluntary matter; it may be that this point, which was clearly of considerable importance, contributed to the eventual disappearance of the register from the Bill in its final form.

Mr Gardham and the Chief Welfare Officer of Bromley, Mr Hanson, were also interested in the question of publicity for, and information about, services available in local authority districts. They sent in examples of the publicity leaflets distributed in their areas. Both Chief Welfare Officers emphasized that the provisions of the then Clause 3, concerned with the provision of special services for the disabled, should be made mandatory. They said that such a provision would be necessary if a more standardized and an improved national service were to be provided rather than a localized and only partially effective one.

A large number of suggestions, including particularly those made by Mr Hilditch, the Chief Welfare Officer of Manchester, concerned the provisions about access to toilets and to public buildings.

The Ministry for Public Building and Works expressed general sympathy with the intention of Clause 6, which concerned access to public buildings.

Some of the more specific Clauses naturally drew a response from bodies particularly affected. The Institute of Chiropodists and the Society of Chiropodists, for example, both welcomed Clause 16, on the provision of a chiropody service for the disabled. The Secretary of the Association of Municipal Corporations, on the other hand, argued that the mandatory provision of chiropody was impracticable because chiropodists were in short supply and there was already a shortage of chiropody services for the present priority group.

The provision of four-wheeled vehicles for disabled people caused a great deal of comment. This was a particularly live issue at the time, as there was a rising tide of concern about the safety of the usual three-wheeled vehicle. The Joint Committee on Mobility for the Disabled submitted detailed figures on the cost of making the change to four-wheeled vehicles and also provided a long memorandum in support of the provision of such vehicles. These provisions were eventually withdrawn from the Bill. There was wide support from many correspondents for the proposals made in Clause 20 to limit the practice of admitting young people to geriatric wards. Alderman Davis and other commentators suggested that the age limit in Clause 20 should be deleted, as it could work contrary to the purpose of the Clause as a whole. This point caused continuing concern throughout the later stages of the Bill; the age limit was, in fact, eventually deleted.

Some Clauses drew adverse comment. Clause 23, on the training of the deaf, was described by the legal advisor to the Department of Education and Science as having no operative effect, partly because it was covered by existing legislation and partly because it imposed no legal obligation at all.

Clause 29, which originally provided for help with meeting the cost of radio licences for disabled people, was generally supported, but a number of people, including the Manchester and Salford Cripples' Help Society and Mr Gardham, argued that in modern society the provision should be extended to television licences as well. This was eventually done.

The Thistle Foundation wrote in to say that it was concerned that the Bill did not extend to Scotland. Alf Morris had deliberately drafted the Bill so that it applied only to England because, as he said, he felt that it would be presumptuous of a mere Englishman to attempt to legislate for Scotland. It became clear in the remaining stages of the Bill, however, that there was general concern that provision in Scotland should not fall behind that in England, and a number of amendments were subsequently introduced to make sure that Clauses of the Bill did apply north of the border.

Numerous suggestions were made for new clauses that might go into the Bill. Most of these were not pursued, but the suggestion of the National Society for Autistic Children for a provision to cover the needs of such children was eventually incorporated into the Bill.

Many correspondents were concerned that the Bill should be made explicitly applicable to mentally handicapped people. Fears that the Bill as drafted did not extend were continually expressed throughout its passage through both Houses of Parliament, despite numerous assurances from Ministers and from Alf Morris himself that the point was adequately covered.

One development of major importance during this period was the setting up of an *ad hoc* committee, comprising Members of Parliament who supported the Bill and members of the Legal and Parliamentary Committee of the Central Council for the Disabled (CCD). The CCD had held a regular meeting of its Legal and Parliamentary Committee on November 20th. The minutes show that Alf Morris's success in the Ballot was reported, and suggestions were invited for incorporation in the Bill. This is a further confirmation of the hurried and informal way in which Alf Morris was compelled to draft the original Bill.

Alf Morris was closely in touch with Mr Duncan Guthrie, the Director of the CCD, whose idea it was to set up the *ad hoc* committee. In a move of crucial importance, he also agreed to provide Alf Morris with some secretarial help, which was desperately needed in order to deal with the very heavy volume of correspondence and with organizational matters. As a result of this generous gesture, Mrs Phyllis Forman, Secretary to the CCD's Legal and Parliamentary Committee, became involved in much of the day-to-day work required by the enormous undertaking of getting a Bill through Parliament. A temporary office was set up at Vincent House, Vincent Square, London, SW1. The Disablement Income Group provided a similar set of facilities for John Astor, who was regarded as the principal Opposition MP involved in support for the Bill.

The Legal and Parliamentary Committee for the CCD held its next meeting on January 5th. By this time Alf Morris's Bill was the major item on the agenda. It was reported to the meeting that Mrs Forman was to act as Secretary to the *ad hoc* committee and as general helper to Alf Morris, and she was congratulated on producing an abstract of the correspondence received by Alf Morris up to that point. Various provisions of the Bill were then considered in detail. Miss Mary Greaves who chaired the meeting of the Legal and Parliamentary Committee and who was also the Director of the Disablement Income Group, reported that she had been invited to Downing Street on January 14th and that she would report to the Committee on any conversation she was able to have with the Prime Minister on the subject of the Bill.

The first meeting of the joint *ad hoc* group of MPs and of the Legal and Parliamentary Committee of the CCD was held in the House of Commons on Wednesday, January 7th. Further detailed consideration was given to the Bill, and a number of issues which were to feature prominently in subsequent discussions in the Houses of Parliament (for example, the question of the Bill's application to the mentally handicapped) were discussed. A further meeting was fixed for January 20th. The pattern was set for a series of meetings, both of the Legal and Parliamentary Committee, meeting regularly as it normally did, and of the joint *ad hoc* Committee, which met roughly once a week throughout the period that the Bill was in Committee.

One important item on the agenda for the meeting of the Legal and Parliamentary Committee on January 16th was the Chairman's account of her meeting with the Prime Minister. She reported that she had found his attitude to be sympathetic and constructive. He had assured her that the Bill would not meet with any obstacle from the Government in its passage through Parliament. This suggests that Harold Wilson had, typically enough, realized the political importance of the Bill, despite Crossman's initial opposition.

This series of meetings of the two committees provided a parallel to the official meetings of Standing Committee C. Many of the same issues were debated, and discussions and conclusions reached in the informal Committees were often reflected in the debates of the Standing Committee. The meetings of Standing Committee C were open to the public, and representatives of the voluntary organizations were in constant attendance to monitor the progress of the Bill and to provide Alf Morris with on-the-spot advice and help as specific points came up. In a Standing Committee of this sort a continuing process of consultation takes place between the Bill's parliamentary sponsors and its extra-parliamentary supporters, with messages exchanged and meetings arranged in the public part of the Committee Room or in the corridor outside.

The first sitting

When Standing Committee C began its deliberations on December 17th Alf Morris immediately introduced,[1] as is customary, a sittings motion, which provided that the Committee should meet again on January 21st (after the Christmas recess) and thereafter each Wednesday morning at 10.30. This motion was immediately put and agreed to; Alf Morris again got to his feet to move a procedure motion,[2] which set out the somewhat unorthodox order in which he hoped that the Committee would agree to consider the various Clauses. As Alf Morris said, he moved the motion 'to meet the convenience of colleagues in the Committee and organizations outside which were advising Hon. Members about various parts of the Bill and because Departments of State required as much time as possible to give a positive response to the propositions which we are making in the Bill'.

The order which Alf Morris had selected was one which was largely forced upon him by the state of readiness of various parts of the Bill. In fact each meeting of the Committee was preceded by a procedural motion which reflected the progress Alf Morris and his colleagues had been able to make in getting various Clauses in the Bill ready for consideration. He was literally drafting the Bill as it went along.

The first Clause moved was Clause 25, which had been drafted by the Ministry of Transport and provided that invalid carriages could be used on the footpaths. There was a reasonably short debate, in which Reg Freeson, speaking on behalf of the Minister of Transport, welcomed the Clause for the Government.[3] He also took the opportunity of declaring his own personal interest in the success of the Bill. The Committee therefore got off to a smooth start with an agreement to approve the Clause.

It is perhaps worth noting at this point that this decision, reached without a division, set the pattern for the remainder of the Committee's proceedings. It was yet another unusual feature of the Chronically Sick and Disabled Persons Bill that at no stage during its passage through Standing Committee was a division called. Even those issues on which some disagreement was expressed the Committee was able to resolve without the formal necessity of proceeding to a vote.

The second Clause considered by the Committee provided an example of the way in which the Committee was able to overcome a lack of agreement. Clause 26 was the provision which Tony Benn had drafted with Alf Morris and which imposed upon the Ministry of Technology a duty to issue an annual report on its work on technology for the disabled. Several members of the Committee, including Laurie Pavitt, Neil Marten and Lewis Carter-Jones, referred to the lack of time which had made it impossible for them to draft and table amendments to the Clause. It rapidly became clear, in any case, that Dr John Dunwoody was unhappy with the Clause because it involved only the Ministry of Technology, whereas his own Department, the DHSS, was that principally responsible for the disabled. He pointed out that the DHSS already published two annual reports, although he conceded that they had not covered the subject as fully as might be desired. He asked whether Alf Morris would be prepared to withdraw the Clause, in view of the fact that, through lack of time, the Departments concerned had not been able to consider it properly. Alf Morris was advised by his backbench colleagues, including Jack Ashley and Dame Irene Ward, that the Clause should not be withdrawn but should remain in the Bill until the Government was able to come forward with an amendment or a new Clause which would meet the point more satisfactorily. The backbenchers thus acted more as a team of negotiators than as members of a normal committee. Alf Morris resolved the difficulty by undertaking to withdraw the Clause on Report, when the Government had brought forward a new Clause to replace it. This was agreed, subject to Neil Marten's proviso that Alf Morris's undertaking should take effect only if the new Clause were regarded as satisfactory.

One of the problems attending the proceedings of the Committee came to a head when the next Clause was discussed. The Chairman's attention was drawn to the fact that fewer than nine members were present and that therefore the Committee was without a quorum. Proceedings were suspended briefly[4] while messages were sent to absent committee members who were no doubt temporarily engaged in business in other parts of the House. Fred Evans took over at this point the role of unofficial whip, and the problem does not seem to have recurred. It is worth noting at this stage that Maurice Macmillan was able to attend only two of the four sessions of the Committee because he was suffering from influenza. He did, however, make a special effort to attend on those two occasions because of his fears that the Bill might otherwise have been delayed.

In its first sitting the Committee dealt with a problem, which arose in relation to Clause 5 and the new Clause which eventually replaced it, that also affected a number of other provisions in the Bill. This was the question of whether the duty to be imposed upon a local authority should be a duty to 'have regard so far as practicable' to the needs of disabled people, or should be in stronger terminology, such as to 'make provision for' the needs of disabled people. The Committee, or at least its backbench members, were extremely concerned that the less strict form of wording gave local authorities too much discretion and in effect deprived the Clause and other similar Clauses of much of their meaning. Fred Evans for example, said in his speech that he would not vote against new Clause 1, but he asked Alf Morris 'to fight as hard as possible to prevent too much discretionary material creeping into the Bill and whenever possible to see that the duties laid upon local authorities are mandatory'.[5] David Weitzman also made the point that but for the shortage of time, he would have tabled an amendment to omit the words 'so far as practicable' because, he said, the Clause meant in law only that benevolent advice was being given to local authorities. The general principle was not resolved at this stage, but the Committee's expression of concern was to bear fruit later.

Another example of the way in which a Committee can work effectively to improve the drafting of a Bill occurred towards the end of the Committee's first sitting. John Astor asked, in relation to the new Clause which required local authorities to have regard to the needs of disabled people in the siting and provision of public toilets, whether this provision also covered toilets in public buildings. He was given a ministerial assurance that a later Clause would cover this point, but when the Committee met again after the Christmas recess the Government had reconsidered its position and conceded that further redrafting would be necessary in order to meet the point.

The second sitting

The second sitting of the Committee was held on January 21st and was again introduced with a procedure motion moved by Alf Morris.[6] The Committee then proceeded to the consideration of a new Clause, drafted by the Ministry of Housing and Local Government and moved by Reg Freeson. The Clause had been reconsidered in the light of John Astor's remarks at the end of the preceding sitting, and Alf Morris acknowledged the sympathetic attitude of the Ministry and the help which Reg Freeson had given both to him and to the Committee. The Committee was still anxious about the use of the words 'so far as practicable'. however, and expressions of concern on this point from all parts of the Committee led the Minister to undertake 'to have another look at it in the light of all the points which had been made'.[7]

An example of the constructive attitude demonstrated by Reg Freeson arose in relation to a further new Clause, dealing with access to toilets for disabled people in public buildings other than those for which local authorities were responsible. The new Clause had been tabled by Alf Morris, who acknowledged in his speech that the Clause would affect the responsibility of a number of Departments other than the Ministry of Housing and Local Government, and he supposed that consultations would be necessary. Reg Freeson was able to tell him that the consultations had already been undertaken[8] and that the Ministries which would be affected, including the Board of Trade and the Ministry of Transport, had already indicated that they did not wish to oppose the Clause. Again, the Minister undertook to look again at the specific phraseology in the Clause when the Bill came back to the House at Report Stage.

By this time, as the formal record of the Committee's proceedings demonstrated, Alf Morris had struck up a good working relationship with the Ministers who were primarily responsible for the Bill. He had regular consultations both with them and with their officials at every stage of the Bill, and his initial feeling that he had been rebuffed by the Government, following his meeting with Richard Crossman, had been by now somewhat assuaged. The Committee was henceforth notable for the number of Clauses and amendments which were introduced formally by the Government (which thereby implicitly undertook some responsibility for the passage of the Bill) or by Alf Morris himself with an acknowledgement that he had had the benefit of Government advice.

An example of this was the discussion on Clause 15, in the Committee's second sitting. This Clause provided that in appointing members of advisory bodies on youth employment, regard should be had to the desirability of including one person with experience of work with young disabled persons. Alf Morris began his speech[9] by saying that he had been 'much helped by the Department with the drafting of this amendment to the Clause as originally planned'. Mr Freeson, replying for the Government, alluded to the fact that 'the proposed amendment Clause has been prepared in consultation with his opposite numbers' in other Departments and that he was therefore glad to say that he could support the Clause.

The third sitting

The third sitting of the Committee, on January 28th 1970, began with yet another procedure motion[10] and then proceeded to consider an amendment to Clause 9, concerning travel concessions for partially blind people. The Clause and amendment were both withdrawn, because, as Alf Morris conceded, he had discovered since drafting the Clause that existing legislation was adequate to cover the constituency case which had prompted it. This brief debate illustrates again the difficulty, because of shortage of time, which Alf Morris had to face in drafting the Bill in its original form.

The help of yet a further Government Department, the Department of Education and Science, was important in the drafting of Clause 31, concerning special education for the deaf-blind, which had been promoted by Jack Ashley. Alf Morris paid tribute both to Jack Ashley's efforts and to the help received from the Department of Education and Science and in particular from the Secretary of State. He was kind enough not to mention that the initial response from the Department had not been so helpful. The Clause, as amended, was welcomed by the Government and was accepted unanimously by the Committee.

A less happy fate befell Clause 22, on discrimination against the deaf in employment, both because its substance was thought to be unnecessary and because it was defective in its drafting. Despite the persuasive speech from its sponsor, Laurie Pavitt, the Committee agreed that the Clause should not stand part of the Bill, though there was some half-hearted talk about the possibility of a better Clause being presented at Report stage.

The important Clause 20, on the admission of young persons in geriatric wards, was replaced in the Committee stage by two new Clauses, which nevertheless retained an age limit, though somewhat extended from the original 45 years of age to a new limit of 50. The Committee was clearly concerned about this point but for the time being accepted the Government's argument that there was no ideal age limit and that, by implication, the age limit specified in the new Clauses was a reasonable compromise.

Alf Morris again had occasion to express his gratitude for the co-operation he had received both from the DHSS and from Parliamentary Counsel when he introduced new Clause 8, which made a number of amendments to the procedure for war pensions appeals. Dr John Dunwoody, for the DHSS, also referred in appreciative terms to the help which had been received from the Parliamentary draftsmen in dealing with this and with other complex Clauses.[11]

An interesting example of the way in which timing may be crucial in amending a Bill in Committee or in adding new Clauses to it arose with new Clause 16, which provided that in appointing members of various consumers' consultative committees regard should be had to the desirability of including at least one person with experience of working with the disabled. This Clause had originally been tabled as new Clause 10, but had reached the Order Paper only on the day before the Committee's second sitting. It had accordingly been starred, to show that it had only just been tabled, and in accordance with a ruling announced by the chairman at the outset of the Committee's proceedings, it was not selected for debate because, in view of its recent appearance, not enough time had been allowed for Committee members to consider its implications. In the event, the Committee did not, in its second sitting, reach the point at which new Clause 10, if selected, would have been considered; Fred Evans, who had tabled the new Clause, was therefore able to move it as new Clause 16 for consideration by the Committee in its third sitting. The Committee did in fact approve the new Clause in a brief debate at the end of its third sitting.

By the end of January Alf Morris had overcome one of the major obstacles to his Bill. He had succeeded in demonstrating to the Government that his Bill was unlikely to go away and that he would persevere with his efforts to pilot it through its remaining stages. As a result, the Ministers affected and the Government in general had come to accept that the Bill would reach the Statute Book and that it would be better in these circumstances, given the growing interest in the measure of the public and the media, if the Government was seen to adopt a sympathetic attitude towards it. This view was of course encouraged by the Bill's supporters in Cabinet, including particularly Fred Peart, a Minister without portfolio.

Cabinet support enabled Alf Morris to overcome what could have been another fatal obstacle. Many of the provisions in the Chronically Sick and Disabled Persons Bill clearly imposed a charge on the public purse. In principle, such charges can only be imposed on a motion proposed by a Minister of the Crown; as we saw earlier,[12] this is an essential safeguard against the introduction by backbench Members of measures which require the taxpayer to subsidize causes of particular concern to the Members' own constituents. If Alf Morris's Bill was to proceed and complete its passage, it would have to be supported by a Money Resolution tabled by a Government Minister.

The fact that the Bill involved the expenditure of public money but was not supported by a Government Money Resolution had been tangentially referred to in the Second Reading debate by Mr A. H. MacDonald. The Bill had nevertheless been given a Second Reading and had proceeded through three sittings of its Committee stage without a Money Resolution, but this was at least partly due to the indulgence of its supporters and others who could otherwise have raised awkward questions. If challenged, Alf Morris could have argued either that until this point his Bill had not proposed any major charges (because the Clauses first considered by the Committee were not those that might impose obligations on local authorities to spend money) or, to the extent that charges were imposed, that they could be met out of locally raised revenue. This would have exploited what was known as the 'Mitchison Gap', named after the Labour MP Dick Mitchison, who had devised the argument that providing expenditure can be regarded as an obligation falling on ratepayers rather than taxpayers, no Money Resolution is required.

The crucial moment would arrive, however, when the major provisions of the Bill (Clauses 1 and 2) were to be considered; there could be no doubt that these Clauses imposed considerable charges on the public purse, and it would be extremely inequitable to allow those charges to be borne wholly by ratepayers. Alf Morris was therefore in the difficult position of needing a Government Money Resolution to cover these provisions if his Bill were to have any chance of success.

Fortunately for him, the Bill's supporters in Cabinet had become aware of this point. Alf Morris recalls that Bob Mellish, then the Government Chief Whip, had arranged a meeting of the various Ministers concerned and had pointed out that it was in the Government's interest, given that the Bill was proceeding satisfactorily, to be seen to be supporting it and that this support would involve the tabling of a Money Resolution. Accordingly, an appropriate resolution was indeed tabled on February 3rd, the day before the Committee's fourth sitting, in the name of Dick Taverne, then a Treasury Minister. The Resolution was drafted in terms which covered the provisions of the Bill to which the Committee had already agreed and, more importantly, it also covered those central provisions at the heart of the Bill to which the Committee were expected to agree in their fourth sitting. The tabling of this Money Resolution marked in a formal sense the Government's support for the Bill and henceforth Alf Morris could be assured that his Bill would, barring accidents, reach the Statute Book.

It was about this time, however, that one particular accident of fortune became likely. The Labour Government was in the fourth year of its term of office, and it was becoming increasingly clear, with the revival of its fortunes in the opinion polls that a General Election was likely to take place in either the summer or the autumn. If the Prime Minister were to opt for a summer General Election, this would necessarily abbreviate the parliamentary session and would place at risk any legislation which had fallen behind in the legislative programme. Henceforth, it was Alf Morris's major preoccupation to ensure that the momentum was maintained and that his Bill did not get bogged down at any stage. As we shall see, he was not always able to convince others of the need for urgency.

The fourth sitting

The chairman of the Committee, Sir Myer Galpern, began the fourth sitting by announcing that a Financial Resolution had been moved relating to new Clause 31 (the main expenditure Clause, which eventually became Clause 2) and that therefore all other Clauses which involved further expenditure and were not covered by the Money Resolution would not be called for debate. Alf Morris had decided, with the informal agreement of the Committee, that the Bill should complete its Committee stage at the end of its fourth sitting. He began on February 4th with the now usual procedure motion;[13] he explained to the Committee that he did not have a compulsive desire for procedure motions but that it was necessary to resort to this practice because of the problems involved in preparing the Bill on his feet.

The Committee then proceeded to a consideration of new Clause 30, which was designed to replace Clauses 1 and 2 of the Bill as originally drafted. Alf Morris moved the new Clause but did so in terms which did not draw attention to its major new feature; instead of requiring local authorities to maintain a register of disabled people, as had been originally required, the new Clause imposed a duty upon local authorities only to take such steps as were reasonably practicable to inform themselves of the number of disabled people in their area. The new Clause was welcomed by Dr Dunwoody, and a brief debate[14] then took place. An attempt was made to raise the question of registration, but the chairman ruled the discussion out of order since it did not arise under the new Clause. Without further comment on this important amendment to the Bill as originally drafted, the Committee approved new Clause 30.

Alf Morris confirms that he was aware that this change was a major one, and that he had been influenced by arguments to the effect that an absolute duty to compile a register would not be compatible with the principle that the placing of names on such a register should be done only with the consent of those involved. He was also concerned about the problem of the confidentiality of information which disabled people might provide to local authorities. For reasons of this sort, Alf Morris was prepared to drop the requirement that a register should be drawn up, but this substantial change and the relaxation of the duty thereby imposed on local authorities was to cause difficulties in the implementation of the Bill when it reached the Statute Book. It must be regarded as part of the price which the Government insisted should be paid if its support was to be offered.

The Committee then moved to consideration of new Clause 31, the provision which eventually became Section 2, which imposes mandatory obligations on local authorities to meet the special needs of disabled people in their areas. In moving the new Clause,[15] Alf Morris referred to an article in *The Times* which commended its provisions and declared that the new Clause would place Britain in the forefront of nations as far as concern and care for the disabled was concerned. This support from *The Times* was typical of the increasing interest which the press generally was showing in the Bill.

In the debate on new Clause 31 another issue which had caused the Committee concern, and which was to reappear on subsequent occasions, was also discussed. This was the question of whether the mentally handicapped were to be included in the categories who were to benefit from the provisions of new Clause 31. Alf Morris made it clear that the new Clause was intended to include them, and this was confirmed by the Minister.

New Clause 32, which replaced Clause 4 of the original Bill, was moved by the Housing Minister, Reg Freeson, reflecting again the extent to which Government Departments had now taken responsibility for the Bill. In moving the new Clause, the Minister referred to the Cullingworth Report, which had been circulated to local authorities and which had dealt specifically with the housing needs of the disabled.

The same Minister was also involved in moving a further new Clause, new Clause 33, which provided that any person undertaking the provision of premises including sanitary conveniences for use by members of the public should have regard, so far as practicable, to the needs of disabled people. This provision was accepted by the Committee in preference to another new Clause, new Clause 11, which had been tabled by John Astor and which went somewhat further in providing that the question of sanitary facilities for disabled people should be taken into account by local planning authorities when they grant planning permission.

The Committee's proceedings were interrupted at this stage by a number of inquiries[16] by members of the Committee concerning the fate of particular amendments or new Clauses which had not been selected. The chairman confirmed that they were not to be called and drew attention to the statement he had made at the beginning of the Committee's sitting to the effect that these were Clauses which involved financial considerations but were not covered by the Financial Resolution and could not therefore be considered. Dame Irene Ward asked whether there was any possibility of amending the Financial Resolution so as to cover these provisions but was told by the chairman that there was no such possibility. Alf Morris intervened to say that, as far as the Clause on chiropody was concerned, an attempt would be made in discussions held between them and the Bill's Report stage to find some way of including that Clause in the Bill.

A potentially important new Clause was then considered. New Clause 12 provided that the terms 'chronically sick and disabled persons' and 'disability' could be defined in regulations made by the Secretary of State and that any such definition should include mental as well as physical disability. The new Clause was tabled and moved by David Weitzman. In his speech on the new Clause the DHSS Minister pointed out the problem that the definitions to be made under the new Clause would apply only to the other provisions of the Bill, and that this could cause difficulties, since many provisions of the Bill in turn depended on provisions in other existing legislation. The Minister, however, recognized the need for further consideration of the point and persuaded David Weitzman to withdraw his Clause on the understanding that discussions would be held to see whether the point could be met.

David Weitzman was also involved in the tabling of new Clause 9, which required the Parliamentary Commissioner for Administration to specify an officer whose specific responsibility it would be to consider matters affecting the disabled. The chairman ruled that this would necessarily involve expenditure and could not therefore be considered, since it was not covered by the Financial Resolution. The Committee concluded its consideration of the Bill by looking at new Clause 34, tabled and moved by Alf Morris, but in fact owing its provenance to Jack Ashley. Again, the Minister felt obliged to say that he was not happy with the wording of the new Clause, which had only recently appeared on the Order Paper. The Committee therefore agreed that while it would approve the new Clause, the Minister would attempt to bring back an improved form of wording at Report stage.

Jack Ashley's role in the Committee is worth noting. He was one of Alf Morris's major advisers on the Bill, and he was an extremely active member of the Committee, despite the handicap of his complete deafness. Fred Evans took on much of the responsibility for sitting beside him and taking notes of discussion which he could not hear; other colleagues on the Committee also took their turns with this task. Jack Ashley writes in his book *Journey Into Silence:*[17]

> The Bill was important to all of us, but two things of personal interest emerged. The first was my friendship with Alf Morris and other Members who worked on the Bill; the second was my close involvement with the passage of the Bill in the House. Alf Morris proved to be a man with quite exceptional understanding of my problem; we soon formed a warm personal relationship which I value highly.... My involvement, entailing much more work than I had anticipated, was exactly what I needed at that time. Working on the Bill pulled me out of the isolation of deafness; it was a pyschological tonic.

By the end of its fourth sitting the Committee had completed its detailed consideration of the Bill and had agreed that it should be reported to the House of Commons as amended, the traditional formula by which a Committee brings its proceedings to an end and propels a Bill towards its next stage. The Bill was returned to the House of Commons so that the whole House could consider it in its new form. Alf Morris briefly thanked the chairman of the Committee, the Ministers involved in the Committee and the Officers of the House, particularly Mr Giles Ecclestone. The chairman had the last word; he expressed relief that the Committee was able to end its deliberations without any further procedure motions!

Report and Third Reading

The Bill had its Report stage and Third Reading on March 20th, which, being a further day allocated for private Members' legislation, was a Friday. Proceedings began shortly after 11 a.m., and Mr Speaker, Dr Horace King, warned that if the work on the Order Paper were to be covered, speeches would have to be brief.[18] This helpful admonition was typical of the concern which Mr Speaker showed to ensure that the Bill did not fall foul of any procedural or timetable pitfalls.

Alf Morris began by moving a new Clause (which eventually became Section 19) concerning the provision by local authorities of information about the availability of chiropody services for disabled people. In this new form the Clause had been deprived of much of its original content, presumably in the interests of saving it from disqualification on the ground that it involved expenditure not covered by the Financial Resolution. Nevertheless, Alf Morris was able to say that the Institute of Chiropodists was extremely pleased at the inclusion of this provision in the Bill.

The House agreed to add this Clause to the Bill but then considered two new Clauses tabled by David Weitzman, one being an attempt to revive Clause 7 of the original Bill, which had been withdrawn during the Committee stage, and the other being an attempt to revive in its original form Clause 21, which had in fact been replaced by new Clause 15 (now Section 16). In both cases David Weitzman agreed to withdraw his new Clauses in the light of disquiet expressed by the Government Ministers involved. These are perhaps examples of the degree to which the backbench supporters of the Bill were beginning to realize the need to jettison certain provisions, which they may well have wished to pursue, in the interests of getting the Bill as a whole through its remaining stages.

The House then accepted two new Clauses. One became Section 22 of the Act and fulfilled an undertaking given by the Minister in the Committee stage to the effect that he would replace the original Clause 26 with a more appropriate provision; the other, which became Section 4, was tabled and moved by Reg Freeson as a comprehensive provision to cover the ground formerly dealt with by three earlier Clauses. Section 4 imposed an obligation on persons providing buildings to whose parking facilities and sanitary conveniences the public has access to have regard to the needs of disabled people.

The subject matter of two unsuccessful attempts at earlier private Members' legislation was revived in a further new Clause moved by Colonel Sir Tufton Beamish. It will be recalled that both Jack Ashley and Gordon Campbell had earlier introduced Bills which would have provided for the setting up of a Disablement Commission;[19] Sir Tufton himself had introduced a Bill which was due for Second Reading on the very day that the Chronically Sick and Disabled Persons Bill was having its Report Stage. Jack Ashley recalled his earlier attempt and expressed surprise that the Government had continued to oppose the proposal, although he acknowledged that there was some provision in the National Superannuation and Social Insurance Bill which would ensure that there were representatives on various advisory committees with special knowledge of the problems of the disabled. Alf Morris confirmed that his original Bill, in Clauses 11 and 30, had contained provisions which had subsequently been taken over by the provisions of the National Superannuaton and Social Insurance Bill; these were the Clauses which provided for an advisory council to supervise the administration of an attendance allowance, and which made special provision to relax the earnings rule for the wives of men who had been drawing sickness benefit for more than 28 weeks. Sir Tufton Beamish sought leave to withdraw the motion, and later in the afternoon his own private Member's Bill was refused an unopposed Second Reading and therefore lapsed.

The vexed problem of definition was at last resolved when David Weitzman moved a new Clause which had gained the support of the Government. In a brief debate the provision which became Section 28 was moved, supported by the Minister and agreed to by the House.

Two new Clauses which covered new ground were moved by Jack Ashley. These eventually became Sections 26 and 27 of the Act and concerned special educational treatment for autistic and dyslexic children. Fred Evans recalled that he had first introduced the problem of autism in his Second Reading speech. Gerry Fowler, for the Department of Education and Science, said that he was happy to accept the new Clauses on behalf of the Government and to commend them to the House. Both were agreed to.

An important group of amendments took as their objective the tightening up of those provisions which allowed local authorities a considerable amount of discretion in carrying out the duties imposed on them. Dr Dunwoody, however, thought that the amendments would raise a number of practical difficulties and might not in any case secure the objective of those who had tabled them. On a vague undertaking from the Government that the matter would be further considered, the amendments were withdrawn.

A further and important group of amendments had mixed fortunes. John Golding moved an amendment to Clause 2 which provided that, in addition to help with wireless licences, help with television licences should also be made available. This amendment was accepted both by the Government and the House. Two further amendments, however, were opposed by the Government and not pressed by the movers; these concerned the redrafting of Clause 2(1)(c) to include the word 'educational' and the addition of 'laundry services' to facilities mentioned in Clause 2(1)(e).

Donald Dewar introduced a group of amendments whose purpose was to reverse the provision excluding Scotland from the Bill unless there were express provision to the contrary. He referred to the fact that Alf Morris had given an assurance in Committee that the provisions of the Bill would be extended to Scotland, and he explained that the Bill's sponsor had never intended to exclude Scotland but had been compelled to do so in the original drafting simply in the interests of speed.

Alf Morris himself confirmed this when he spoke, and he referred to the help he had received from the Secretary of State for Scotland and the Parliamentary Under-Secretary in that Department. Mr Bruce Millan, the Parliamentary Under-Secretary, added the Government's support to the amendments, which the House approved.

A constructive attitude on the part of the Government was again manifested by Reg Freeson, when he moved an amendment to Clause 4, which as it stood required any person undertaking the construction or equipment of any building to 'have regard' to the needs of disabled people. The amendment instead obliged such persons to 'make provision' for the needs of the disabled. Alf Morris again welcomed the help he had received and the strengthening of this provision.

The House returned to another matter which had caused great

concern throughout the stages of the Bill up to this point. In the Clauses dealing with the separation of younger from older patients, anxiety had been expressed over the best way of defining the two groups. The Clause as originally drafted had specified an age limit of 45 year and in Committee this had been extended to 50 years. At Report stage Arthur Latham, acting on behalf of Will Griffiths, who had tabled the amendment, moved an amendment which struck out the age limit altogether. Alf Morris referred to a number of individual cases which illustrated the importance of the Clause. He paid tribute to the work of Mr and Mrs Marsh Dickson and urged the Government to look at the problem sympathetically.

Dr John Dunwoody, for the Government, agreed that this was 'one of the most sensitive and one of the most difficult issues in the Bill'[20]. He recognized that the use of an age criterion was liable to be arbitrary and unsatisfactory. He concluded by saying that he would give an undertaking that if the amendment were withdrawn, he would reconsider the matter with a view to introducing a suitable amendment in the House of Lords. This was accepted. A number of further and relatively minor amendments were made, and the Report Stage was concluded just before 3 p.m.[21]

Alf Morris then had the pleasant duty of moving that the Bill be read a third time. He began by recalling his Second Reading comment, that the Bill was very much a 'collective essay'. He said that it had been much improved by its examination in Committee and by the further debates at Report stage. He referred to the help he had received from the All-Party Disablement Group and in particular from Jack Ashley and John Astor. He also thanked the individuals and voluntary organizations involved in supporting the Bill, particularly Mr Duncan Guthrie and Mrs Phyllis Forman, the Central Council for the Disabled, the National Campaign for the Young Chronic Sick, Miss Mary Greaves and the Disablement Income Group. He again thanked Mr Giles Ecclestone for his help in drafting the Bill and in facilitating its passage through the Committee.

In what may now be seen as a prescient passage in his speech, he referred to suggestions that there should be a Minister for the Disabled. He referred to this suggestion only for the purpose of expressing his thanks to Dr Dunwoody and Reg Freeson, whom he described as 'joint Ministers for the Disabled'. He expressed the particular pleasure which he felt at the passage of Clause 23, on war pensions appeals, since his own father had died from his war wounds.

Other speakers expressed their admiration for the way in which Alf Morris had guided his measure thus far. John Astor also referred to the valuable groundwork which had been done by the Disablement Income Group. John Page acknowledged that the Bill had prompted MPs 'to put our own house in order' by asking the Serjeant-at-Arms to see whether the House could be made more accessible to disabled people. Fred Evans referred to a *Daily Telegraph* editorial which made the point that the Bill was only a start and that much remained to be done.

For the Government, Dr John Dunwoody was lavish in his praise of Alf Morris. He pointed out that it would have been easier for him to choose a less complex and shorter subject. Instead, 'he selected what I think is the Private Member's Bill of the year. Every year in Parliament there is one Private Member's Bill which goes down in Parlimentary history. In years to come people will remember this year as the year of the Bill to which we are now about to give a Third Reading.'[22]

Laurie Pavitt referred to the help which the police and other servants of the House had given to those disabled people who had attended the Committee stage. Jack Ashley paid tribute to the help the sponsors had received from the Government: 'All the work which has been put in by the Government has not been visible. It has been like a duck's feet. They have been paddling away like mad, but the work has not been visible in the House.' He concluded by saying, 'What the Bill has done is to focus the public mind and the minds of Hon. Members on the general problems over a vast range of disablement.' The Bill was given a Third Reading before the end of the day's business at 4 p.m.[23]

The Bill had therefore successfully completed its passage through the House of Commons and, barring accidents, was now assured of passing on to the Statute Book. It had secured vital Government support, both in the drafting of its provisions and in the tabling of the Financial Resolution, and the growing interest from the media and the public ensured that there could be no back-tracking in the Government's support.

The House of Lords

On the other hand, there was still the House of Lords to negotiate.

This seemed unlikely to offer significant opposition to the Bill, but it did mean that unless the Bill could be piloted through the House of Lords with the minimum loss of time, there was still a danger that the Bill might be lost if a summer General Election should truncate the parlimentary session.

Therefore, at the same time as arranging a small party in the House of Commons on March 24th to thank the Bill's supporters and to mark its passage through the House of Commons, Alf Morris and his administrative assistant, Mrs Phyllis Forman, set about organizing matters in the House of Lords. An approach had already been made to Lord Longford, a former leader of the House of Lords, who had agreed to take responsibility for the Bill in the Upper House. Dozens of letters were sent out to members of the House of Lords whose attitude to the Bill was thought to be sympathetic. Many names were obtained from the letterheads of voluntary organizations working in the field of disablement. A number of sympathetic members of the House of Lords were identified and invited to the reception in the House of Commons on March 24th. The other guests included the members of the Standing Committee, other backbench supporters, civil servants who had been involved, members of the press and representatives of the voluntary organizations.

The joint *ad hoc* Committee had continued to meet throughout the passage of the Bill in the House of Commons. It had been joined in its meeting of March 3rd by four members of the House of Lords, an indication that even at this stage Alf Morris was looking forward to, and planning for the further stages in the Upper House. It was announced at this meeting that Lady Serota would leading for the Government and was willing to meet a body representing the joint *ad hoc* Committee.

A meeting organized specifically for Members of the House of Lords was held on March 25th. Fourteen peers were present, together with three Members of the House of Commons, including Alf Morris, and representatives of voluntary organizations. Lord Longford took the chair and arrangements were made for the proceedings in the House of Lords. A number of peers offered to speak in debates on particular subjects, and some consideration was given to amendments and new Clauses. Jack Ashley raised the question of how far amendments would be pressed, given the pressure of time.

The Bill had its Second Reading in the House of Lords on April 9th.[24] Lord Longford moved the Second Reading[25] and said how proud he was to do so at the invitation of Alf Morris. He also remarked, somewhat ominously for those who had hoped for a speedy passage through the Lords, that the Bill would need strengthening in important respects. He was concerned, for example, at the words 'reasonably practicable' in Clause 1, which he felt qualified too much the duty imposed on local authorities. He was also anxious to tighten up the definition Clause and raised again the question of whether the Bill covered the mentally handicapped.

The second speaker in the debate was Lord Sandford, who in effect spoke for the official Opposition.[26] He welcomed the Bill and recalled that a number of backbenchers had attempted to legislate on the subject in the recent past. He expressed mild surprise that the measure had not been introduced by the Government itself and said that he had noticed that the Bill had been pretty severely 'knocked about' in the Committee stage, thirteen of its thirty-three Clauses having been removed altogether. He also expressed concern about the problem of definition.

Baroness Serota spoke for the Government early in the debate.[27] She remarked upon the widespread support which the Bill had obtained and on the number of Government departments affected by the Bill. She said, however, that neither she nor, she believed, the Ministers concerned would be in favour of handing these responsibilities over to a Ministry for the Disabled.

On the question of definition, she expressed a preference for avoiding sharp dividing lines and described Clause 24 (eventually Section 28) as a longstop measure which would enable the Secretary of State to make definitions where necessary. She was also able to assure Lord Longford that the Bill covered mentally handicapped people.

The first of four maiden speeches was made by Baroness d'Arcy de Knayth.[28] The Baroness's speech was notable not only for the fact that it was her maiden speech, but also because she was herself disabled and confined to a wheelchair. In all, four disabled Members of the House of Lords made speeches in the debate. Baroness Masham of Ilton also made her maiden speech from her wheelchair, as did Viscount Ingleby. Lord Crawshaw made up the quartet of disabled peers whose presence necessitated a physical rearrangement of the furniture in the House of Lords' Chamber. (The crossbenches had been removed so that the disabled peers could have room for their wheelchairs.)

The extent to which the Members of the House of Lords still hoped to extend substantially the provisions of the Bill was exemplified in the speech of Lady Masham.[29] She referred in particular to the problem of mobility for disabled people and the special problems of paraplegics and tetraplegics – the spinal-injury cases.

Lord Wells-Pestell, who had himself been disabled earlier in life, also expressed concern at the discretionary element in Clause 1. He was strongly of the view that these obligations must be made mandatory. The Duke of Atholl asked why Clauses 1 and 2 did not apply to Scotland; he was unimpressed by the argument that Section 12 of the Social Work (Scotland) Act, 1968, covered the ground. This point was supported by Lord Drumalbyn. The debate was concluded by a short speech from Lord Longford, who expressed his gratitude to the Government for its constructive attitude and repeated that he hoped that the Bill could be considerably strengthened. He acknowledged, however that there was a limit to the extent to which the Bill could be transformed. The bill was given a Second Reading and committed to a Committee of the whole House.[30]

The Lords' Committee

The first meeting of the House of Lords Committee[31] on the Bill took place three weeks later, on April 30th. The Committee immediately returned to an issue which had caused concern throughout the proceedings in the House of Commons. Lord Amulree moved an amendment which would leave out of Clause 1 the words 'to take such steps as are reasonably practicable'. He argued for the amendment that would close any such loophole. In what Lord Longford described as 'a most unpleasant surprise', Lord Sandford, speaking for the Conservative peers, argued against the amendment on grounds that local authorities had little idea of who the disabled were, how many there were of them and how much it would cost in time and effort to draw up a register.[32] Baroness Serota, for the Government, took a more favourable attitude, however. She recommended the Committee to accept the amendment, in the hope that the Clause would then stand 'as a clear line of guidance to all local authorities', although she expressed the hope that a similar attitude would not be taken to the words as they appeared in other Clauses.

The second major issue was the subject of the second amendment, moved by Lord Wells-Pestell. He attempted to introduce into Clause 1 the obligation for local authorities to prepare a list, within twelve months of the passing of the Act, of all disabled people. This was a reversion to Alf Morris's original idea of a register, an idea which had been quietly dropped in the later stages of the House of Commons Committee proceedings. On this occasion, Baroness Serota advised the Committee against the amendment. She was concerned about the practical difficulties of imposing an obligation to draw up a 100 per cent register, and she also believed that such a provision would take the Clause beyond the terms of the Financial Resolution and would therefore involve a question of privilege, since only the House of Commons has the constitutional power to put forward measures involving public expenditure. Lord Wells-Pestell, following the reluctant advice of Lord Longford, agreed to withdraw the amendment.[33]

An interesting side-light on the degree to which the Government had by now accepted responsibility for the Bill was cast by the discussion on the next amendment. The amendment confirmed the requirement that local authorities should inform disabled people of the services available to them. A small dispute arose as to whether the Bill as drafted extended the obligation to those disabled people who were not actually using the services; Baroness Serota attempted to defuse this issue by conceding that the sponsor of the Bill, Lord Longford, was likely to know more about its meaning that she was. Lord Longford replied, somewhat sharply, that 'though this Clause must come before the House on my responsibility, it would be totally misleading – and we really must not be misled by this – to suggest that this has been worked out without reference to the Government draftsmen.'[34]

One of the factors which was increasingly in the minds of the Bill's supporters was, of course, the impending likelihood of a General Election. Lord Oakshott intervened to 'enter a cautionary word about the Parliamentary programme'.[35] He said: 'This is a very good Bill – a very good Bill indeed. Let us not strive too hard for perfection. I appeal to your Lordship's Committee to accept a modicum of imperfection because I think that otherwise we run a grave risk of losing the Bill altogether.' Lord Longford refused to accept any such view. He conceded that he had read in the *Daily Telegraph* that 'the peers were in some danger of destroying this Bill' but was unimpressed by this: 'I repudiate that prospect utterly. This Committee must be allowed to do its duty.' He saw no chance of the Bill's being lost through lack of time. Lord Leatherland weighed in on the side of Lord Oakshott. He pointed out that there were 53 amendments on the order paper, and that if 20 or 30 of them were carried, the House of Commons would then have to spend considerable time on considering those amendments. 'I sincerely hope we shall concentrate on the main issue, and that is to get the Bill passed.'

This exchange shows that the Bill's supporters and sponsors were becoming increasingly worried at the prospect that it might be 'killed by kindness'. It was clear that there were still many in the House of Lords, including some of the Bill's closest friends, who were concerned to improve or extend it, but who, with the best of intentions, might inadvertently jeopardize its passage through delay. While this prospect was a relatively remote one as long as Parliament ran a full session, the likelihood of a summer General Election meant that less time might be available than had been hoped. Alf Morris was in touch with Fred Peart and others in the Labour Cabinet and was well aware of the increasing likelihood of a prime ministerial announcement that a General Election would be held.

The House of Lords Committee, however, continued to give detailed consideration to a number of amendments and new Clauses, including those designed to extend to public transport the obligation to consider the needs of disabled people and to make mandatory the provision of information about aids and applicances to those who prescribe them for disabled people.

Baroness Masham of Ilton successfully moved the short but important amendment which extended the Clause concerning equipment to enable disabled people to use telephones to the provision of telephones themselves.[36] Two minor improvements were made to Clause 2; after brief debates the words 'educational' was inserted before 'facilities' and the criterion of safety was also added to those of 'comfort and convenience'.[37]

An attempt to introduce a major new principle into the Bill was made by Lord Mais. He moved an amendment imposing on local authorities providing accommodation for chronically sick and disabled people the obligation to pay them an equivalent sum if they did not wish to live in that accommodation. Although the amendment commanded the wholehearted support of Lord Longford and other peers, Baroness Phillips, for the Government, pointed out that the National Superannuation and Social Insurance Bill was a more appropriate measure for providing this type of benefit and that it already made provision for an attendance allowance. There was also the problem that the amendment would go beyond the terms of the Financial Resolution. In the face of these arguments, Lord Mais agreed to withdraw the amendment.

Baroness Masham introduced a new Clause which would require a doctor to certify, in appropriate cases, that a patient was suffering from disabling neck or back injuries. She was particularly concerned with this point, as a victim of such injuries herself, because she believed that early treatment and diagnosis in these cases were absolutely essential. Baroness Serota, however, while declaring the Government's sympathy with the objective of the Clause, advised the Committee to reject it on the ground that it was very difficult to interfere with the kind of clinical care which doctors believed was appropriate in individual cases. Baroness Masham agreed to withdraw the amendment but gave notice that she might introduce it, in a redrafted form, at Report stage.

A small but important point was the subject of an amendment to Clause 4, moved by Lord Crawshaw. He argued that where special facilities were made available for disabled people, they should be adequately signposted and publicized. Lord Kennet, for the Government, while expressing sympathy for the aims of the amendment, pleaded that he had only just seen it on the Order Paper and had not been given time to consider a proper response. However, he undertook to look at the question sympathetically before Report stage.

The Government was a little better prepared in respect of a similar amendment concerning Clause 5, on the subject of the provision of toilet facilities. Lord Hughes, a Scottish Minister, moved three amendments to this Clause on behalf of the Government, all of which were accepted by the Committee. Lord Crawshaw was therefore able to withdraw his own amendment to Clause 5.

The Committee accepted a further group of amendments, moved by Baroness d'Arcy de Knayth, which provided not only that various advisory committees should include at least one person with experience of work among disabled people, but that regard should also be had to the desirability of including a chronically sick or disabled person.

A similar principle animated a new Clause moved by Lord Longford, providing that local authority committees with responsibilities towards the disabled should have regard to the desirability of co-opting a chronically sick or disabled person to their membership. This new Clause became Section 15 of the Act.

The Committee returned to the vexed question of the age limit which would define those young patients who were not to be admitted, under the provisions of Clause 14, to geriatric wards. Lord Amulree moved an amendment which would strike out the age limit altogether. This attempt had been made in the House of Commons but had been resisted by the Government. On this occasion, however, the Government had had second and better thoughts, and Baroness Serota was able to welcome the amendment, which was accepted by the Committee. Thus, the longest-running saga of the whole Bill was brought to an end in a manner wholly satisfactory to its backbench sponsors.[38]

Baroness Masham introduced a new Clause which would extend and standardize the special provisions made by local authorities to help disabled people to park their vehicles. Lord Hughes, for the Government, proposed that if the new Clause were not pressed, he would undertake to table an amendment at Report stage which would secure her objective. Baroness Masham agreed.

Lord O'Hagan moved a further new Clause, which revived one of the provisions of the Bill in its original form, that concerning the provision of vehicles for haemophiliacs. The original Clause had not been moved in Standing Committee in the House of Commons, and it made little advance on this occasion. Baroness Serota said that the Government was unwilling to single out special groups for help in this way, and that she was unable to accept the amendment. A similar fate befell other amendments which introduced the question of the replacement of the three-wheeled invalid carriage by a four-wheeled vehicle. These were withdrawn by their movers after Baroness Serota had explained that their financial implications made it impossible for the Government to accept them.

The Committee rose shortly after 10 p.m., Lord Longford remarking that the Committee had done good work for about seven hours and that it was now an appropriate time to adjourn.

What is remarkable about the Committee stage in the House of Lords at this point was the extent to which the Bill was still being subjected to major amendments and to the introduction of substantial new Clauses. The initial lack of professional expertise and of time in the drafting of the Bill was still being reflected in the degree to which its original provisions needed constant rewriting and amendment. A further factor was the nature of the Bill itself; it was a kind of 'omnibus' on to which could be loaded almost any piece of luggage which was thought to be of benefit to the disabled. As a result, there was the constant temptation felt by well-meaning supporters of the Bill to add just one more provision to deal with an issue dear to a particular heart which had not been included in the original scope of the Bill.

This process was viewed with increasing alarm by the Bill's friends. Expressions of concern appeared in the press. The Guardian of May 5th issued a warning, and on May 9th the paper published a letter from Mr G.A.G. Brooke of the CCD, warning that the Bill was in danger of being lost through delay in the House of Lords.

By the time the Committee next met, on May 15th, the atmosphere had changed somewhat; the likelihood of a General Election had become much stronger. Lord Longford intervened early in the Committee's proceedings to say that 'it would be idle not to face the fact that we are very close to a general election'; he went on to say;

> If nothing particular had been done about this Bill, it would simply have been lost, because the Report stage would have been due during the period of this hypothetical election. I must therefore express my gratitude to the Government for helping to facilitate its passage and agreeing to give time next Wednesday afternoon.[39]

Lord Longford was here referring to a decision which had been taken in the Cabinet as to the legislation which would assume priority if a General Election were called. Perhaps influenced by a leading article in the *Sunday Times,* which had urged the Government not to allow the Chronically Sick and Disabled Persons Bill to founder, the Cabinet had agreed that the Bill should proceed and that special provision should be made for it to ensure that it would not fall through lack of time. Ironically, one of the victims of the shortage of time was the National Superannuation and Social Insurance Bill, the major measure promoted by the Department of Health and Social Security, whose fortunes Richard Crossman had been so keen to protect when Alf Morris had first raised with him the possibility of his own private Member's Bill.

Lord Longford recognized the new situation. He still warned against 'unconditional surrender' and was careful to say that he was 'not suggesting that there should be some perfunctory dismissal of the Bill' but he did concede that 'we should not behave and fight on as though nothing had happened.' The position was spelled out even more clearly by Lord Sandford, who declared, 'The whole Bill is now imperilled by the possibility of an early election, and it seems quite clear to me that every amendment moved against the better judgement of the Government imperils it still more.' Baroness Serota wholeheartedly agreed.

The Committee was not deterred from trying to introduce yet more provisions into the Bill, however. Lord Raglan moved an amendment which would create a special division within the DHSS to deal with the problems of disabled people and which would, incidentally, strike out of the Bill those provisions which dealt with specific groups of disabled people, such as the autistic and dyslexic.

Lord Longford, now convinced of the need for speed, sprang to the defence of these provisions: 'These particular kinds of disablement were given a priority as a result of all those discussions. I think it would be the greatest mistake in the world to try to undo that work. It would certainly finish off the Bill.' He added that he was not in favour of a Ministry for the Disabled. He was strongly supported in this by Baroness Serota. The amendments were withdrawn.

When one of the Clauses which had been under attack from Lord Raglan, Clause 20 dealing with the Institute for Hearing Research, came up for discussion the attack was renewed, but Lord Segal carried the day when he remarked, 'As a matter of expediency and in order to get this Bill passed through with the minimum of delay, we should not seek to alter the Bill by wholesale deletion of these Clauses.' Nevertheless, a major attack was made on the phrase 'early childhood psychosis', which appeared in the provision concerning autistic children, but Lord Segal, the mover of the amendment, was persuaded to withdraw it.

The last issue dealt with by the Committee was one that, despite constant ministerial assurances, had bothered the Bill's supporters almost from the outset. Lord Longford moved an amendment to Clause 24, the definition Clause, to provide that the expressions 'chronic illness' and 'disability' should include chronic mental disability. The point was met by Baroness Serota when she undertook to ensure that in any circular issued after the Bill had come into operation it would be made clear that the needs of the mentally handicapped were to be covered by the provisions of the Bill. Lord Longford agreed not to press his amendment, and the Committee stage concluded.[40]

As Lord Longford had earlier remarked, the Government had made special provision to provide time for the Bill's Report stage and Third Reading. This took place[41] less than a week later, on Wednesday, May 20th, and the House of Lords was able to dispose of a number of the points which had been the subject of ministerial assurances at earlier stages. These included provisions which became Sections 8 and 21 of the Act. Section 21, concerning the use of badges for display on motor vehicles used by disabled persons, originated in a new Clause moved by Lord Hughes on behalf of the Government. This provision, involving public expenditure, raised an issue of privilege which was dealt with later by the House of Commons.

Even at this late hour, however, further attempts were made to introduce new provisions into the Bill that had not been agreed with the Government. Baroness Masham returned to her special concern about the treatment of patients with spinal injuries. She introduced a new Clause which would require patients suffering such injuries to be transferred to a specialist centre within 24 hours. In moving the new Clause, she recognized that this was 'the eleventh hour of the Bill'. As with a similar amendment at Committee stage, Baroness Serota declined to accept it on behalf of the Government because she maintained that it would interfere with the clinical judgement of doctors. Lord Longford intervened to say that while he was not at all persuaded by this argument, he would nevertheless suggest to Lady Masham and to the new Clause's supporters that they should not press this amendment. He did so 'for one reason only – a reason of time and situation .... I feel that there would be a danger to the Bill if this amendment were pressed.'[42]

The final stages

Despite the House's sense of urgency and its now manifest willingness to abandon Clauses dear to many hearts in the interests of the survival of the Bill as a whole, further time was lost owing to a procedural confusion when the House had concluded its Report stage and the Third Reading was moved.[43] When the Deputy Speaker put the motion that the Bill should be read a third time, Lord Longford rose to move formally. No one else rose to speak and the Deputy Speaker was therefore obliged to put the question that the Bill be read a third time. The Third Reading was carried without a division.

Lord Longford then rose to say that he had not achieved his purpose. He had hoped that peers would have an opportunity to say a few words on Third Reading. A long procedural wrangle then took place, and Lord Shackleton, the Government's leader in the House of Lords, was compelled to intervene. It was argued that since a number of those peers who wished to speak on Third Reading were confined to their wheelchair, it had been extremely difficult for them to leap to their feet in order to catch the Deputy Speaker's eye! Lord Shackleton eventually suggested, in response to a comment by Earl St Aldwyn, that the Deputy Speaker might put the question again. Harmony and order were thus restored, and a short debate on Third Reading took place.[44]

Lady Masham remarked, in a brief contribution, that she had found it most interesting to see the two front benches supporting each other over the Bill. Baroness Serota, for the Government, said that it was 'a remarkable Private Member's Bill, remarkable in its length for a Private Member's Bill, and remarkable for its scope, and also perhaps most remarkable for the enthusiasm which it had received both inside and outside Parliament'.

The last word lay with Lord Longford. He thanked the Government Ministers concerned and observed, 'There will be a duty on the Government, which I hope and believe they will fulfil, to interpret this Bill as humanely and liberally as possible.'

The end of the long parliamentary journey was now in sight. The Prime Minister had announced on May 18th that there was to be a General Election on June 18th. The parliamentary session was therefore rapidly coming to an end, but the passage of the Bill was now assured. All that remained was a brief consideration by the

House of Commons of the amendments which the House of Lords had made.

The House of Commons attended to this business on May 27th. Alf Morris, in moving that the House of Commons agree with the Lords' amendment deleting from Clause 1 the words 'take such steps as are reasonably practicable', took the opportunity of expressing his gratitude for the help he had received from Lord Longford in the House of Lords.[45] He also thanked Baroness Serota and her ministerial colleagues and the civil servants who had been involved in the Bill. He paid tribute to the work of Mr Giles Ecclestone in the Public Bill Office and also to the help he had received from Mr Julian Elliston, Parliamentary Counsel, who had died just before the Report stage in the House of Commons.

The House then proceeded to agree to the Lords' amendments and new Clauses. In the case of the new Clause providing for a scheme of badges for display on motor vehicles used by disabled persons, the Speaker was obliged to call the attention of the House to the fact that privilege was involved. This point arose because of the 'sole and undoubted right of the Commons to impose taxation', and the new Clause, having been introduced in the Lords, could be said to infringe this principle. In such circumstances the action open to the Commons is either to disagree with the amendments on the ground of privilege, or to agree with them, waiving privilege *pro hac vice*. If the latter course is decided upon, a special entry is made to this effect, and that is what happened on this occasion.[46]

The proceedings in the House of Commons concluded when Jack Ashley moved that 'the House doth agree with the Lords' amendment' which provided for the coming into force of different provisions of the Act on different days. At the conclusion of Jack Ashley's short speech. Mr Speaker remarked that it was appropriate that Mr Ashley, 'who has triumphed so magnificently over his disability' should 'speak on this amendment, which is the last in the Bill'. The last word was left to Dr John Dunwoody, who paid tribute to all Members who had worked so hard on the Bill and particularly to Alf Morris.[47] The Bill received the Royal Assent on May 29th 1970.

NOTES

1. *House of Commons Select Committee C Debates,* 1970 (hereafter *H. C. S. C. Deb.*, 1970), col. 3.
2. ibid.
3. *H. C. S. C. Deb.*, 1970, cols. 9 – 10.
4. *H. C. S. C. Deb.*, 1970, col. 34.
5. *H. C. S. C. Deb.*, 1970, col. 40.
6. *H. C. S. C. Deb.*, 1970, col. 47.
7. *H. C. S. C. Deb.*, 1970, col. 57.
8. *H. C. S. C. Deb.*, 1970, col. 62.
9. *H. C. S. C. Deb.*, 1970, col. 90.
10. *H. C. S. C. Deb.*, 1970, col. 95.
11. *H. C. S. C. Deb.*, 1970, col. 140.
12. See p. 19.
13. *H. C. S. C. Deb.*, 1970, col. 145.
14. *H. C. S. C. Deb.*, 1970, cols. 145 – 50.
15. *H. C. S. C. Deb.*, 1970, col. 151.
16. *H. C. S. C. Deb.*, 1970, col. 178.
17. Jack Ashley, *Journey into Silence*, Bodley Head, London, 1973, p. 175.
18. *H. C. Deb.*, vol. 798, col. 831.
19. See pp. 5-6.
20. *H. C. Deb.*, vol. 798, col. 905.
21. *H. C. Deb.*, vol. 798, col. 910.
22. *H. C. Deb.*, vol. 798, col. 922.
23. *H. C. Deb.*, vol. 798, col. 928.
24. *H. L. Deb.*, vol. 309, cols. 239 – 315.
25. *H. L. Deb.*, vol. 309, col. 239.
26. *H. L. Deb.*, vol. 309, col. 246.
27. *H. L. Deb.*, vol. 309, col. 254.
28. *H. L. Deb.*, vol. 309, col. 267.
29. *H. L. Deb.*, vol. 309, col. 272.
30. *H. L. Deb.*, vol. 309, col. 315.
31. *H. L. Deb.*, vol. 309, col. 1115.
32. *H. L. Deb.*, vol. 309, col. 1117.
33. *H. L. Deb.*, vol. 309, col. 1126.
34. *H. L. Deb.*, vol. 309, col. 1133.
35. *H. L. Deb.*, vol. 309, col. 1136.
36. *H. L. Deb.*, vol. 309, col. 1155.
37. *H. L. Deb.*, vol. 309, cols. 1151 – 2.
38. *H. L. Deb.*, vol. 309, col. 1209.
39. *H. L. Deb.*, vol. 310, col. 840.
40. *H. L. Deb.*, vol. 310, col. 872.
41. *H. L. Deb.*, vol. 310, cols. 1085 – 118.
42. *H. L. Deb.*, vol. 310, col. 1095.
43. *H. L. Deb.*, vol. 310, cols. 1106 – 111.
44. *H. L. Deb.*, vol. 310, col. 1112 – 18.
45. *H. L. Deb.*, vol. 810, col. 2005.
46. *H. L. Deb.*, vol. 801, col. 2010.
47. *H. L. Deb.*, vol. 801, col. 2015.

CHAPTER FIVE

The Act: Legislative and Parliamentary Consequences

The passage of the Chronically Sick and Disabled Persons Bill through all its stages was a remarkable parliamentary triumph. That triumph was made all the more noteworthy by the fact that the Bill was unusual in a number of respects, and that its unusual features added to the parliamentary difficulties. Unlike most private Members' Bills, it had been drafted from scratch and in haste by its sponsor. It was longer than most private Members' Bills and certainly covered a much wider scope. It involved the responsibilities of eleven or twelve Government Departments. At the start it encountered hostility from the major Department involved, but eventually it depended on Government support, both because of its financial implications and because it had to overcome the constraints of an abbreviated parliamentary session.

The fact that the Bill ultimately attracted a good deal of Government support raises the question of why such an important measure was not initiated by the Government in the first place. On the face of it, a measure of such complexity and importance seemed an unlikely candidate for private Members' legislation and would have been more appropriate as part of a Government legislative programme.

Perhaps the major reason that a measure of this sort was not promoted by the Government, and was unlikely to be, was precisely the fact that it involved the responsibilities of so many Government Departments. In the nature of the Whitehall process, legislation is much more likely to be generated and given impetus if it is the sole or major responsibility of one particular Government Department. Alf Morris's measure was so wide-ranging that no one Department could have been expected to launch it. Taken individually, each of its provisions might well have been expected to appear in other pieces of legislation, but a comprehensive measure of this type could only have been drafted by someone outside the Whitehall machine. This perhaps partly explains the Government's initial coolness; its subsequent endorsement of Alf Morris's objectives reflected its adjustment to the idea of a multi-departmental measure of this sort.

The success of the exercise to get the Bill on the Statute Book also raises a further question. As we have seen,[1] a number of backbench Members had unsuccessfully tried on earlier occasions to introduce measures of a more limited nature in the field of disablement. Why did Alf Morris succeed where his predecessors had failed?

The answer is a complex one. First, Alf Morris was presenting his Bill under Standing Order No. 6, rather than under Standing Orders Nos. 37 or 13, and this meant that he had an advantage over at least some of his predecessors. There was also the psychological significance of the fact that Alf Morris had come first in the ballot. The person who heads the list in the ballot naturally attracts a good deal of attention. Expectations are aroused, and success is more or less assumed.

Those earlier backbench attempts at legislation had in any case partly exemplified and partly reinforced growing interest in the disabled in political circles. By the time Alf Morris had decided to legislate, public and parliamentary awareness of the problems of the disabled had reached an unprecedented level, and it could be argued that the time was therefore ripe for legislation; only the mismatch between the subject matter of the Bill and the division of responsibilities in Whitehall had inhibited a comprehensive look at the problem, and a backbencher in Alf Morris's position could be said to have arrived at the right point at the right time.

Of perhaps more crucial importance was the fact that Alf Morris was able to construct a remarkable alliance of parliamentary and public opinion to support his Bill. His own experience and knowledge was, of course, crucial. His personal commitment and determination must have weighed very heavily in the balance in the early stages of the Bill; a less determined politician may well have been deterred by Government opposition and by the sheer enormity of the task before him. He was able to draw upon the knowledge, advice and support of the voluntary organizations which had become prominent in the preceding years and on the parliamentary skill and help of the members of the All-Party Disablement Group. The fact that he was able to draw upon this help from many quarters strengthened his position and signalled to all those in Whitehall and elsewhere who might otherwise have doubted his seriousness of purpose that the Bill would not fail through want of wide-ranging support.

The role of the media was important as well. The national press generally welcomed the legislation and took a close interest in it as it made its progress through both Houses. Newspapers like the *Sunday Times* and the *Daily Telegraph* wrote leading articles in support of the Bill; *The Times* published an article by its sponsors; and other newspapers, such as the *Guardian*, opened their letter columns to those who wished to express opinions in its favour.

All of these factors persuaded the Government to take an increasingly favourable attitude towards the Bill. Quite apart from those members of the Cabinet who may have supported the Bill for its own merits, there were others, particularly Fred Peart, who no doubt felt a personal commitment to the Bill by virtue of their relationship with Alf Morris. This support was immensely valuable as the session drew to its premature close and the Bill had to compete with the Government's own legislation for the limited time available. It also meant that Alf Morris was increasingly able to draw upon official help and expertise in drafting the provisions of the Bill and thus to supplement the help which he obtained from parliamentary colleagues like David Weitzman and from staff of the House like Mr Giles Ecclestone.

The difficulties which the DHSS increasingly found with its own major piece of legislation, the National Superannuation and Social Insurance Bill, may also have helped. By the time the Chronically Sick and Disabled Persons Bill reached its crucial stage, it was clear that the Superannuation Bill was in serious difficulties; it may be that the DHSS recognized then that Alf Morris's Bill represented at least a chance that something to the credit of the Department could be rescued from the parliamentary bog into which the major Bill had fallen.

Nor was it simply a question of support from the Government party that mattered. The Chronically Sick and Disabled Persons Bill benefited enormously from the fact that it enjoyed all-party support and that in both Houses the official Opposition endorsed the Bill's major objectives. Indeed, it may well be that the assurance which Alf Morris received from the Conservative leadership to the effect that his Bill would immediately be enacted in the event of a Conservative victory in the General Election spurred the Government on to demonstrate its own enthusiasm for the measure.

Without taking too cynical a view, it seems likely that Alf Morris also benefited from the developing pre-electoral competition between the major Parties. The measure clearly had wide popular appeal and could be presented as an indication of the Government's concern for the disabled, notwithstanding its prominence as a private Member's measure. There were therefore positive electoral arguments in favour of Government help for Alf Morris in the later stages of the Bill, and there were correspondingly powerful arguments against the Government's attracting the odium of being seen to frustrate or destroy the Bill.

The Bill's passage was significant in other respects. Its all-party support, and the fact that the Bill required continual redrafting as it made its progress through the various stages, combined to demonstrate the great advantages, in some cases at least, of a non-adversary approach to legislation. While Parliament will always be dominated by measures of a contentious nature, where it is entirely appropriate and beneficial that the Government should propose and the Opposition oppose, there are other instances when a genuine Committee approach to a piece of legislation may produce valuable results. The Chronically Sick and Disabled Persons Bill is an example, and it clearly benefited from the constructive and co-operative approach evinced by its supporters on all sides of both Houses. The debates in the Committee stages in both Houses compare very well with the usual sterility and time-wasting of Standing Committees on Government legislation. In the case of the Chronically Sick and Disabled Persons Bill it may fairly be said that the Committee fulfilled its proper function in considering the Bill in detail, so that it more effectively achieved the objectives of its sponsors. There seems little doubt that the example provided by measures such as the Chronically Sick and Disabled Persons Bill increased the dissatisfaction and frustration which many Members of Parliament felt about the inadequacies of the Standing Committee procedure in the case of Government legislation, and this led in turn to the recommendations of the Select Committee on

Procedure in 1978 designed to improve the operation of Standing Committees.[2]

The Bill may also be regarded as the seedbed for a number of ideas which later bore fruit. One of its major achievements was, of course, simply to focus attention on the disabled and to alert those in Whitehall and in local government to the special needs of the disabled and the responsibilities which Government bears in this respect. Subsequent improvements in the rights of the disabled in respect of mobility and income may clearly be said to have stemmed from the awareness of disablement which Alf Morris's Bill stimulated. Other developments were also foreshadowed. The possibility that Government responsibility for the disabled should be placed in the hands of a single Minister was frequently canvassed at various stages in the Bill's progress. The fact that a Minister for the Disabled was eventually created, and that that Minister should be Alf Morris himself, was a peculiarly fitting by-product of the Act. Other ideas also surfaced, including the notion that an ombudsman for local government and for the Health Service should be set up; even the House of Commons itself was persuaded to improve access for the disabled by extensively adapting its buildings as a result of the involvement of disabled people in the passage of the Bill.

One of the most direct consequences of the Bill was the modification of parliamentary procedure itself. The Select Committee on Procedure, sitting in March 1971, considered the whole question of private Members' legislation with a view to making recommendations on improving the rules which govern it. On March 21st 1971 Alf Morris was invited to give evidence to the Committee and was examined on his experience in piloting the Chronically Sick and Disabled Persons Bill through Parliament.[3] The chairman of the Committee was concerned to know whether Alf Morris had had any help in the drafting of his Bill. Alf Morris outlined the difficulties that he had encountered. The chairman asked whether he felt that the parliamentary draftsmen could help a Member who was to introduce a private Member's Bill. Alf Morris replied that the availability of a parliamentary draftsman would have been considerable help in his own case. He pointed out that in the later stages of his Bill he had received increasing help and attention from parliamentary draftsmen and the legal staff of many of the Departments involved.

He was then asked if it might have been helpful if the ballot had been held earlier, perhaps before the beginning of the summer recess. Alf Morris replied that this would not have been as helpful as it might seem at first sight, because it was essential that in drafting his Bill he should be in close contact with his parliamentary colleagues and others whose availability could only be guaranteed while Parliament was in session.

It was then suggested to him by John Mackintosh that he had been 'too kind', that he had been left by the Government Departments to carry the burden himself, and that he had, in fact, been in the rather unusual position of having to produce a Bill unaided. John Mackintosh suggested that the machinery of the House did not provide facilities for people in that position. He concluded that if Members intended to take private Members' legislation seriously, the procedural rules and lack of resources meant that they were ill-equipped to do so.

Alf Morris confirmed in response to a later question, that time had been his biggest problem. In answer to a question from Willie Hamilton, he said that his difficulty in agreeing to the general availability of drafting assistance for every private Member wishing to bring forward a Bill was that some 70 or 80 private Members' Bills a year are introduced, many of them simply for propaganda purposes. As he pointed out, there was no need in such cases, any more than in the case of Parliamentary Questions, that they be expertly drafted. John Parker suggested that in the case of a Bill which obtained a Second Reading, however, drafting assistance should be provided, and Alf Morris readily agreed.

He concluded by making the point that confining private Members' legislation to Fridays constituted an additional burden, since this was the day on which it was difficult to persuade Members to remain in the House when they had obligations in their constituencies.

As a partial response to Alf Morris's evidence, the Select Committee in its Report[4] made a number of recommendations, some of which were acted upon and some of which were not. It suggested that the ballot should be held before the summer adjournment, but this recommendation has not been taken up. They further recommended that a private Member should be permitted to introduce a balloted Bill in the House of Lords and subsequently bring it to the Commons; this too has remained a recommendation only.

The Committee did make one recommendation, however, that stemmed directly from the evidence which Alf Morris had given. In paragraph 56 of the Report the Committee says:

> Some time, at present wasted, would be saved, especially in Committee and on report of private Members' Bills, if drafting assistance were available before Second Reading to private Members winning a high place in the ballot....Your Committee believe that it is right that the Government should provide some drafting assistance for private Members, particularly if the ballot is held earlier in future.

As a result of this recommendation, the House passed a resolution[5] to provide up to £200 worth of drafting assistance to the first six Members in the private Members' ballot.

In overcoming the peculiar difficulties involved in putting his Bill on the Statute Book, Alf Morris made it easier for his successors to follow in his footsteps. Fascinating though it may be as an exercise in parliamentary procedure, the Bill's real significance lies in its subject matter. For the first time a comprehensive measure to benefit the disabled had been enacted; it remained to be seen how effective its implementation was to be.

NOTES

1. See pp. 5-6.
2. Select Committee on Procedure, *First Report*, 1977-78, House of Commons, 588 – i.
3. Select Committee on Procedure, *Second Report*, 1970 – 71 House of Commons, 297 – v.
4. ibid.
5. *H. C. Deb.*, vol. 827, col. 209.

CHAPTER SIX

Help for Handicapped People before 1970

Before the passing of the Chronically Sick and Disabled Persons Act 1970 most of the help offered to disabled citizens was provided under legislation which had not been framed with disabled people specifically in mind.

For example, many disabled people were handicapped in earning a living and were therefore among those who had received assistance under the various Poor Laws. Such help was given, however, in order to relieve their destitution, and their disability, while it may have caused their poverty, was only an incidental factor in their qualifying for assistance. The first real legislative recognition of the special needs created by disability came late in the nineteenth century with the passing of the Elementary Education (Blind and Deaf Children) Act 1893. This was followed in 1899 by an Act facilitating special educational provision for mentally subnormal children, and the Education Act 1918 which required local education authorities to make special educational provision for all handicapped children who needed it and who were not so severely mentally subnormal as to be judged incapable of benefit.

After 1918 the major concern with handicapped people shifted from disabled children to focus on the needs of the thousands of crippled ex-servicemen. In 1919 Government legislation set up training centres for the war disabled, in order to retrain them in suitable skills to enable them to obtain civilian employment, and incentives were offered to employers to recruit a proportion of their work force from disabled ex-servicemen. An Act of 1920 extended these facilities to blind civilians.

The economic recession of the 1920s and 1930s not only largely defeated the purpose of the above measure, leaving many disabled unemployed, but also meant that no further provision was made for disabled people until the Second World War had started. In 1941, faced with an acute shortage of labour for the war industries since all the fit young men had been conscripted into the armed forces, the retraining facilities were extended to all civilian disabled.

Towards the end of the war, in 1944, the Disabled Persons' (Employment) Act was passed, establishing assessment opportunities and industrial rehabilitation and retraining services for all disabled people who were judged to have employment potential, irrespective of the cause or circumstances of their disability. After this piece of legislation, which was reviewed in 1957 and was reported to be operating in a generally satisfactory manner,[1] little more was done specifically for disabled people until the Chronically Sick and Disabled Persons Act, 1970.

Uneven provision of services

During the years since the end of the Second World War, local authorities had developed supporting services for disabled people under the National Assistance Act 1948. This Act included a section (Section 29) which permitted local authorities to offer a number of services to those of their citizens who were in need by virtue of age or infirmity. Under this section some local authorities had provided their disabled citizens with social and leisure opportunities, holidays, meals-on-wheels, home adaptations, televisions or telephones. The organization of such services was permissive, not mandatory, and local authorities varied widely in the extent of provision made for disabled people under this section.

There were considerable differences between authorities in the energy displayed to identify and register disabled citizens as a preliminary to informing them of available services. The London borough of Southwark, for example, with a population of 290,530, had, by 1969, registered 994 as blind or partially sighted, 377 as deaf or hard of hearing and 4669 persons with other mental or physical handicaps.[2] Even this total of 6040 disabled persons was almost certainly an underestimate of the true extent of handicap in the borough, since a survey conducted by the Office of Population

Censuses and Surveys in 1969 revealed that there were three million physically handicapped and impaired persons living in private households in Britain. This indicates that 3 per cent of the population is disabled, whereas Southwark's figures for registered disabled in 1969 suggested only 2 per cent. Southwark, however, was very much nearer the 3 per cent figure than Cambridge County Council. That authority, with a population size similar to that of Southwark, had registered only 588 blind or partially sighted persons, 141 deaf or hard of hearing and 658 persons with other handicaps. This amounted to less than 0.5 per cent of the population and clearly reflected the lack of enthusiasm on the part of Cambridge County Council for identifying its disabled citizens rather than a real difference in the prevalence of handicap in Cambridge as compared with Southwark or the nation as a whole.

There was even greater diversity in the amounts of money spent by local authorities on each of the people whose names they placed on the general handicap registers. The Isle of Wight, for example, spent 16 shillings per person registered in 1969, while the London borough of Southwark, with eighteen times as many disabled people registered out of a total population less than three times as large as that of the Isle of Wight, spent £51 12 shillings a head, 64 times as much money on each handicapped person.[3]

The very great and inequitable disparity of local authority provision for handicapped people prompted Alf Morris to strengthen local authority obligations in his Chronically Sick and Disabled Persons Act 1970, and Section 2 of the Act made mandatory the provision of a number of forms of assistance to people whose disability created special needs.

The National Assistance Act also required local authorities to make residential care available to any elderly or disabled persons who could no longer manage, by reason of infirmity, to live in a private household. Again, there was great disparity of provision between authorities. Some chose to build their own residential units especially for disabled people; others accommodated disabled people of all ages and elderly people together; yet others opted to pay maintenance changes for any of their citizens for whom they accepted responsibility in a home run by a voluntary charity or sometimes in a privately run profit-making home.

There was less variation between local authorities in the rate of expenditure on residential accommodation in respect of the elderly, children in care and the handicapped combined, although the most generous provision was at a rate four times higher than that of the lowest. The official statistics in the period up to 1970 do not permit a breakdown of the figures to consider expenditure on residential care for disabled people alone. Even the numbers of handicapped people in residential care were not accurately known until after the passing of the Chronically Sick and Disabled Persons Act. From the information which was available at the time, it appears that by the mid-1960s there were some 4500 physically handicapped people under 65 years of age in local authority residential accommodation, and at least as many again were sponsored by local authorities in voluntary or private homes. There were also 5000 or 6000 mentally handicapped persons in residential accommodation (as distinct from hospitals), most of it local authority accommodation.[4]

By no means all these handicapped people were in units geared to their special needs. For many individuals the only residential care available was in a home primarily concerned with the care of elderly persons. It was in order to meet the need for residential care places for the younger physically handicapped that the Cheshire Homes developed and became the largest non-statutory provider of residential accommodation for physically disabled people. The first Cheshire Home was founded in Hampshire in 1948 by Group Captain Leonard Cheshire, VC, and the number of homes grew rapidly in the following years, each one starting up as a result of local initiative to meet a need that the statutory authorities were not satisfying. By 1970 there were 64 Cheshire Homes in Britain, accommodating some 1700 handicapped people, and by 1980 this number had grown, at a slower rate in recent years, to a total of 74 homes, with about 2000 residents in total.

The early vigorous development of voluntary residential provision for handicapped people reflects the slow initial response of local authorities to the need for residential care units specially for younger disabled people. The energies of local authorities were mainly taken up with making provision for the growing numbers of elderly infirm, and the unfortunate young person who was severely handicapped and unable to live at home, and for whom no vacancy could be found in a voluntary home, was often condemned to endure years of miserable existence in units of elderly people. The plight of such younger disabled, imprisoned in geriatric units, gained increasing publicity in the 1960s and was very much in the mind of Alf Morris when he framed the Chronically Sick and Disabled Persons Bill.

The awakening of parliamentary concern with welfare services, as distinct from employment services for disabled people, was marked by a request from a backbencher to the then Minister of Pensions (Iain Macleod) in 1955 to make sufficient resources available to local authorities to enable them all to provide adequate services for disabled people.[5] The response was that a Committee was already in being to consider the matter. This was the Committee of Inquiry chaired by Lord Piercy that reported in 1957 but confined itself (as, indeed, its terms of reference required) to reviewing the employment opportunities of disabled persons. In 1959 the issue was again raised in the House of the very uneven local authority provision of welfare services for disabled people, but once again the response was non-commital − the local authorities were to be requested to do better in future.[6]

Concern about the welfare of disabled persons grew during the 1960s, which were years of increasing affluence for the majority, serving to emphasize the disadvantages suffered by the disabled minority. From the parliamentary session of 1964 − 65 onwards, it is evident from the volume of references in Hansard to matters concerning disabled people that there was much more, and better organized, pressure for the improvement of services.

Much of the impetus for this came from the Disablement Income Group, a pressure group founded in 1965 by Megan du Boisson, herself disabled. The Group established contact with a number of sympathetic Members of Parliament and peers from each of the three main parties, stimulating them to table repeated questions about provisions for handicapped persons. The Disablement Income Group, as its name implies, was concerned primarily with improving financial provision for disabled people. Its declared aim was to obtain a disablement income for all handicapped people, one that was geared to the degree of disablement and was payable irrespective of the circumstances in which disablement occurred.

Financial support for disabled persons

At the time the Disablement Income Group was formed (and still today) only war disabled and industrially disabled persons received pensions in respect of their disability in amounts that were related to the extent of disability. These pensions were payable irrespective of any other earned or unearned income which the claimant might have and represented a form of compensation for loss of function caused by disability. The Disablement Income Group was formed to campaign for the extension of this type of financial provision to include all disabled, however the disablement had occurred. The majority of disabled people become disabled in adult life as a result of disease unrelated to employment or war service. For these people the only financial benefits are those to which they may be entitled under Social Security pension schemes or from Supplementary Benefit.

The National Insurance Act 1946 made provision for Sickness Benefit to be paid to those insured workers temporarily unable to work because of ill health. It was envisaged as a short-term benefit to tide people over the interruption of earnings occasioned by sickness. The need for long-term support of permanently handicapped people was not really considered when the National Insurance Act was framed, presumably because it was assumed that, with free health care, only very few people would fail to recover from illness and would be unable to return to work. In default of any other provision, Sickness Benefit was drawn indefinitely by those insured workers who remained too disabled to return to employment. The level of benefit was, however, ungenerous as a permanent income, and the regulations required periodic recertification of incapacity, which was an additional cause of complaint. In 1971 a new National Insurance benefit, the Invalidity Benefit, was introduced, payable to insured workers who, after exhausting their six-month entitlement to Sickness Benefit, remained incapacitated for employment.

Even in 1971, however, no provision was made for two other groups of disabled people whose plights were mentioned more and more frequently after 1965. The Disablement Income Group had from its inception, highlighted the difficulties of the disabled housewife and of the person disabled from birth or early childhood who had never been able to work and thus had never built up a National Insurance contribution record. For congenitally disabled people there was only National Assistance (renamed Supplementary Benefit in 1966), which was payable to disabled and able-bodied alike who had no other means of support. The disabled housewife usually received no financial support at all, either from National Insurance or from National Assistance/Supplementary Benefit, even if she became so severely handicapped that she could not carry out essential housekeeping duties and had to pay for domestic assistance to keep her family together. The disabled housewife's ineligibility for benefit was a consequence of the fact that few married women, even if they took up paid employment outside the home, paid full National Insurance contributions. Most elected to pay the reduced rate of contribution, which covered the risk of industrial injury only and entitled them to no other benefits. A married woman worker paying reduced contributions who subsequently became too disabled to work was not therefore entitled to Sickness Benefit or to the Invalidity Benefit when it was introduced. Neither, as a married woman living with her husband, had she any right to claim Supplementary Benefit, since she was deemed to have adequate means of support through her husband's earnings or pensions and allowances.

The lack of help available to the severely disabled housewife was a matter for which the Disablement Income Group obtained considerable publicity in the years after 1965, but it was not until 1977 that any financial benefit was available to disabled housewives (other than the Attendance Allowance introduced in 1971) and even then it was not on a scale to satisfy the demands of the Disablement Income Group.

Although the financial difficulties of disabled people were increasingly acknowledged in the late 1960s, the Chronically Sick and Disabled Persons Act, as a private Member's measure, was subject to the limitation that it could make no provisions which would commit the Government to large-scale expenditure. None the less, when Alf Morris first began the task of drafting his Bill he considered the possibility of trying to introduce an attendance allowance.

The idea of such an allowance for civilian disabled, similar to that payable to war disabled who needed considerable personal attention, had been raised early in 1964.[7] The Government then rejected the suggestion, claiming that an attendance allowance 'would be an alien benefit in a ...National Insurance... system which gives benefits in respect of loss of earnings',[8] but by 1966 the possibility of introducing such an allowance was being officially investigated. It was linked with the desire to offer some financial assistance to severely disabled housewives. While the Chronically Sick and Disabled Persons Bill was in preparation, the Government introduced into its National Superannuation and Social Insurance Bill provision for an attendance allowance, and Alf Morris dropped the item from his measure. In fact, the former Bill was lost when the Labour Government fell in 1970, as we have noted, but the succeeding Conservative government introduced the attendance allowance in 1971 as part of its social security legislation.

Other issues concerning the welfare of disabled persons which cropped up frequently in parliamentary questions and debates, revealing increasing awareness on the part of the legislature of the problems of disablement, included the availability of mechanical aids, access to buildings and public transport for disabled people, their need for special housing provision and the unsuitable residential care accommodation offered to many younger handicapped persons.

The Chronically Sick and Disabled Persons Act

The years between 1965 and 1970 were a time of increasing public awareness of the needs of disabled people, reflected in the greater press coverage of issues related to handicap. Even more significantly, the legislature was having its attention focused on specific areas of need. In this way, a climate of opinion was being created which acknowledged that the personal tragedy of disablement could and should be mitigated by the provision of services and financial benefits. Evidence was relentlessly accumulating to prove that the system then current led to uneven, inadequate provision which compounded the functional loss of disablement with gross but avoidable social disadvantage.

It was in this atmosphere of concern about the welfare of disabled people that the private Members' ballot of 1969 was held, and Alf Morris drew first place. His choice of subject for his Bill, and even the specific Clauses of the Bill represented a culmination of several years of pressure and publicity about the problems of disablement.

The general aim of the Bill was to make it obligatory for local authorities to provide persons with the services which they had permissive powers to provide under the National Assistance Act.

The Bill also sought to ensure that all local authorities were at least as energetic in discovering and meeting the needs of their disabled citizens as the best authorities had been under existing legislation. Consequently, the first section of the measure, when enacted, required each local authority to inform itself of the number of disabled persons in its area and to acquaint any such persons with the services available relative to their needs. The types of welfare service which local authorities were to provide were listed in Section 2 of the Act, while Section 3 required local authority housing departments to have regard to the special needs of disabled persons when making their plans for future housing developments. Sections 5 to 8 inclusive dealt with various aspects of access for disabled persons. Sections 9 to 15 inclusive were designed to ensure that disabled individuals themselves were part of the membership of councils or committees involved in matters affecting disabled persons. Sections 17 and 18 required the National Health Service and local authorities to provide statistics showing the numbers of chronically sick and disabled persons under 65 years of age who were accommodated in units devoted wholly or mainly to the care of elderly persons. The remaining sections of the Act dealt with miscellaneous matters such as the use of mechanically propelled wheelchairs outdoors, special parking facilities for disabled persons, research into aids and equipment, local authority statistics on special educational facilities for certain categories of handicapped children, and the interpretation of terms used in the Act.

It was a wide-ranging measure, touching on most of the issues, other than financial support, which had figured prominently in the growing volume of discussion about the welfare of disabled people. At this point, some ten years after the Chronically Sick and Disabled Persons Act reached the Statute Book, it is time to assess the contribution it has made to improving the lives of disabled people.

It is possible to discern three main areas within which the Act sought to promote the wellbeing of disabled people. The first is the identification of handicapped people and the provision of information about services available; the second is the provision by each local authority of personal social services; the third is housing and access for, and participation of, disabled persons in the community.

The next three chapters will deal with each of these areas in turn, followed by some concluding remarks which attempt to evaluate the overall significance of the Chronically Sick and Disabled Persons Act 1970.

NOTES

1. *Report of the Committee of Inquiry on the Rehabilitation, Training and Resettlement of Disabled Persons* (the Piercy Report), Cmnd 9883, Vol. XIV, 1955-56.
2. *Welfare Services Statistics, 1969 – 70*, Institute of Municipal Treasurers and Accountants and the Society of County Treasurers, 1970.
3. ibid.
4. *H. C. Deb.*, vol. 751, col. *1401*.
5. *H. C. Deb.*, vol. 544, col. 805.
6. *H. C. Deb.*, vol. 596, col. 200.
7. *H. C. Deb.*, vol. 689, col. *836*.
8. ibid.

CHAPTER SEVEN

Identifying Disabled People

Section 1 of the Chronically Sick and Disabled Persons Act 1970 imposed a duty on local authorities to ascertain the numbers of disabled people in their respective areas in order to provide supporting services for them. In the view of many, the task of discovering the numbers and circumstances of disabled people logically came prior to the development of services to meet the needs of such people.

Some years earlier, in 1965, Mrs Shirley Williams had asked in the House for information about the numbers of disabled people not in receipt of any financial benefit in respect of their disablement; she was told that such information was not available because the total number of disabled people in society was unknown.[1] During the next two years other Members of Parliament sought information about disabled people, and again the information was not available.[2] At the end of 1967 a Government spokesman announced that the Office of Population Censuses and Surveys had been asked to undertake a study to ascertain the numbers of substantially and permanently handicapped adults living in private households. It was also reported at the same time that a survey of younger chronically sick and disabled people in hospitals and residential care was already in progress.

The need for more information about the numbers and circumstances of disabled people as a preliminary to organizing services for them which were appropriate and adequate was, therefore, already recognized by the time the opportunity was presented to Alf Morris by the ballot to frame a private Member's Bill to make further provision for the welfare of chronically sick and disabled persons.

The structure of his Act gives priority to the obligation to compile information about the needs of disabled people. In fact, however, Section 1 did not come into operation until thirteen months after most of the rest of the Act, and provision for this delayed enforcement was written into the measure from the beginning. The reason for postponing the enforcement of a duty widely seen as a necessary preliminary to the development of supporting services was simply that the social services departments of local authorities, which would have had to carry out the practical exercise of compiling information about disabled people, were being reorganized. The Seebohm Report on the personal social services[3] had recommended a number of changes in the organization of local authority welfare services, and a new form of social services department was being worked out (it was established in 1971). Until these new departments became operational, it was not considered practicable to insist on the implementation of Section 1 of the Chronically Sick and Disabled Persons Act. There seems to have been general agreement on this point between the sponsors of the Act and the Conservative Government which had to implement the measure when it took office in 1970, immediately after the Act received the Royal Assent.

Although one or two questions were asked in Parliament about the date when Section 1 would come into force, the explanation that this would not be until late in 1971 was readily accepted. A greater cause of concern with regard to this section became apparent early in the parliamentary session of 1970 – 71 and was in respect of the way in which local authorities might interpret their obligations under this section.

The interpretation of Section 1

Just after being returned to power, the Conservative Government had issued a circular of guidance (Circular 12/70) to all local authorities on the implementation of the Chronically Sick and Disabled Persons Act 1970. In this communication it was once again noted that Section 1 of the Act would not come into force until the new social services departments had been established, but the point was made that when the section was implemented, local authorities would be required to inform themselves adequately

> of the numbers and needs of substantially and permanently handicapped persons in order that they can formulate satisfactory plans for developing their services .... It is *not* a requirement of the section that authorities should attempt 100 per cent identification and registration of the handicapped. This would be a difficult, expensive and time consuming exercise, diverting excessive resources from effective work with those who are already known ....[4]

The circular suggested that the report of the survey conducted by the Office of Population Censuses and Surveys would enable local authorities to make a preliminary assessment of the need for services. The report referred to was, in fact, published in the spring of 1971,[5] six months before Section 1 came into force. Its main findings were already known in Government circles by 1970, when the circular was dispatched. The figure suggested by the Office of Population Censuses and Surveys of 1,200,000 severely or appreciably handicapped people living at home, of whom the majority received no supporting services at all, raised Government fears that any energetic attempt at 100 per cent identification of disabled individuals would stimulate a demand for services which resources were utterly inadequate to meet.

When Circular 12/70 referred to the report of the national survey as being sufficient to enable local authorities to make a preliminary assessment of need, and emphasized that 100 per cent identification of the handicapped was neither expected nor desirable, concern began to be expressed by the sponsors of the Chronically Sick and Disabled Persons Act. They argued vehemently that if local authorities were encouraged to think that sample surveys could produce the information that Section 1 of the Act required them to collect, the real objectives of the section would be missed, since handicapped people could not thus be individually identified.

In March 1971, in a question in the House about the implementation of Section 1 and the possibility of sample survey techniques being used by local authorities to discharge their obligations, Alf Morris said, 'It would be the merest academic exercise to find out numbers if we are not able to identify the severely disabled who need help.'[6] It seems clear that at this stage Alf Morris and other supporters of the Chronically Sick and Disabled Persons Act regarded Section 1 as requiring local authorities to identify individually each disabled person and his or her needs in order to be able to offer to specific individuals the service or services which would afford them the greatest help.

While drafting his Bill, Alf Morris had been fully aware of the survey being conducted by the Office of Population Censuses and Surveys, and knew as he framed Section 1 of his Bill that the survey report[7] would indicate overall numbers of handicapped people broken down into regions. It is true that the regions into which the country was divided in the report of the national survey did not coincide with the boundaries of local authorities either before 1974 or after reorganization in that year, but if, at the time of the Bill's passage, it had been intended to compile for each local authority area the information that had been gathered nationally, the wording of Section 1 could have made this fact clear. Indeed, it is possible that the Office of Population Censuses and Surveys could have analysed its data on the basis of local authority areas or groups of local authorities instead of, or in addition to, analysing on the basis of regions.

There can be no doubt, therefore, that the original intention of Alf Morris was that local authorities should identify, person by person, the handicapped individuals in their respective areas. His categoric rejection, as 'the merest academic exercise', of any interpretation of the section in the form of an assessment of overall numbers confirms that this was again his view in 1971. Others, both inside and outside the House of Parliament, had expected that the implementation of Section 1, even as finally worded, would lead to a list of names and addresses of disabled people in each local authority area and information about their need for services.

None the less, despite these clear expectations, Sir Keith Joseph, who was Secretary of State at the DHSS at the time, directed local authorities towards making an assessment of numbers rather than individual identification. Just before Section 1 came into force in October 1971, a circular went to all local authorities from the DHSS[8] giving guidance on the execution of their responsibilities under the section.

The circular referred to the report of the national survey of handicapped people carried out by the Office of Population Censuses and Surveys, a copy of which had been sent to each local authority on publication. The circular suggested that unpublished survey material indicated so much variation in the prevalence of handicap in selected local authority areas that the national figures could not serve as a reliable guide to the need of any individual area. For this purpose, information needed to be gathered locally, and the circular recommended this should be by means of a local sample survey on the lines of the national survey. Enclosed with the circular was a booklet which had been prepared for the purpose by the Office of Population Censuses and Surveys at the request of the DHSS, entitled 'Sample Surveys in Local Authority Areas with particular reference to the Handicapped and Elderly'.

It was acknowledged in the circular that a sample survey would not fulfil 'the ultimate task of identifying everyone who both needs and *wants* a service', but the view was expressed that few authorities would feel able to embark on a programme of identifying all such people. Indeed, the circular went further and commented pointedly: 'it appears to the Secretary of State that the cost and effort of making inquiries of each household in the authority's whole area may result in so great a diversion of resources that the whole purpose of the task would be nullified.' In case this warning proved insufficient to discourage authorities from attempting 100 per cent identification, the circular also emphasized the danger of arousing in disabled people an expectation of services which the local authority would find itself without resources to provide.

It seems clear that the findings of the national survey of handicapped people living at home had served as both a stimulant and a brake on the development of services to meet the needs of disabled people. The figure of three million permanently impaired people, one third of them substantially handicapped in performing basic day-to-day activities, had certainly highlighted the need for supporting services. Greater public awareness was reflected in the increased space devoted to matters concerning disabled people in the national press, and the increased time given in both Houses of Parliament to issues related to the welfare of handicapped persons. At the same time, the particular provisions of the Chronically Sick and Disabled Persons Act were looked at in a new light when the numbers of potential beneficiaries became known. This was particularly true of Section 1 and of Section 2, which imposed a duty on local authorities to meet the needs of the disabled individuals whom they identified in respect of practical assistance, leisure opportunities, home adaptations and holidays. As the sheer size of the potential commitment became known, so the interpretation of those provisions of the Chronically Sick and Disabled Persons Act in a way commensurate with the ability and willingness of the community to provide resources became a matter of crucial importance.

The actual wording of the Act had been deliberately imprecise in a number of instances. For example, the terms 'chronically sick' and 'chronic sick' and 'disability' and 'disabled' were not defined anywhere in the Act, although provision was made in Section 28 of the Act for regulations to be drawn up by the Secretary of State, if he should think it necessary, defining these terms in respect of any service which could be provided. (So far, no such regulations have been made.) Moreover, nowhere in the Act is there any clear statement of what would constitute a need on the part of a chronically sick or disabled person for any particular service.

This lack of precision may well have facilitated the passage of the Bill, enabling it to complete all the necessary stages to reach the Statute Book before the dissolution of the Government in 1970. It most certainly created a situation in which the administration charged with putting the measure into effect was exposed to charges of bad faith and callous expediency in its interpretation of the Act. This was particularly true with regard to the implementation of Sections 1 and 2, yet it is difficult to argue either that a different administration would have made different decisions, or that the way in which the wording of the Act was interpreted was a distortion of the true meaning of the words – although it may not have been the interpretation which the sponsors of the Bill had hoped for when they agreed to the imprecise wording.

With regard to Section 1, for example, despite Alf Morris's rejection of local sample surveys of handicapped people as valueless 'academic exercises', he could not deny that the wording of the Act would bear such an interpretation. The section says:[9]

1 (1) It shall be the duty of every local authority having functions
        under section 29 of the National Assistance Act 1948 to inform
        themselves of the number of persons to whom that section
        applies within their area and of the need for the making by the
        authority of arrangements under that section for such persons.

As has been argued above, when this section of the Act was being drafted Alf Morris undoubtedly had in mind some sort of inquiry of each household in each authority's area in order to identify handicapped individuals whose needs it would then become the authority's duty to meet under Section 2 of the Act. Even if a Labour Government had been returned in the 1970 election, it is likely that that administration also would have been dismayed by the immensity of potential need revealed by the national survey of handicapped people living at home, and would have shrunk from too energetic a search for disabled individuals who might need help and support. Whatever administration had been in office, it is likely that Section 1 would have been interpreted in the way that Sir Keith Joseph suggested. Support for this view comes from the fact that when a Labour Government was returned in 1974 and Alf Morris was appointed to the newly created post of Minister with special responsibility for disabled people, there was no firm instruction to local authorities to embark on a programme of individual identification of handicapped persons if this had not already been done. Even the reorganization of local government in 1974 did not prompt new guidance from the Minister for the Disabled to local authorities, although information about handicapped people which had been collected by the old authorities could not immediately be related to the newer, larger areas which were created in 1974.

The problems of compiling registers of disabled persons

By this time, of course, there had been an opportunity to examine the implications of Section 1, not only in the light of the knowledge of the large numbers of handicapped people in the community and the relative scarcity of resources, but also on the basis of the experience of local authorities in trying out various methods of assessing the needs of their disabled populations. A survey of the way in which local authorities discharged their obligations under Section 1 was begun by the Department of Social Administration of Birmingham University in 1973. This revealed that despite Circular 45/71 of September 1971, with its clear discouragement of attempts to locate handicapped individuals, a surprising number of local authorities still proceeded to carry out some sort of household inquiry. The distribution of the main methods of inquiry used by local authorities in the execution of their duties under Section 1 of the Chronically Sick and Disabled Persons Act, 1970 is shown in table 1.

TABLE I   *Methods used by local authorities to assess numbers and needs of disabled people*[10]

Nos. of local authorities*	Method of inquiry†
69	House-to-house distribution of leaflets with tear-off slips to be returned by anyone who was substantially and permanently handicapped
37	Sample survey on the lines suggested in the booklet prepared by the Office of Population Censuses and Surveys
32	Other sample surveys
19	Miscellaneous other methods
157	

*The information is not complete for all pre-1974 local authorities.

†Where a local authority employed a combination of methods of inquiry, for the purpose of this table it is classified under the method which formed the main part of its inquiry.

The Birmingham University report[11] on local authorities' efforts to implement Section 1 of the Act came to the pessimistic conclusion that in general the inquiries had added little other than confusion to the known picture of need. The writers accepted that a number of the sample surveys were soundly organized and efficiently carried out, but felt the information obtained was not markedly superior to that which could have been derived from the national survey findings of the Office of Population Censuses and Surveys. On the other hand, the investigation had shown that many of the house-to-house inquiries were methodologically defective, and that the findings yielded were of doubtful validity. In most of these inquiries, handicapped people were asked to complete a form with details of (at least) the nature and degree of handicap, and the age, sex and household composition of the respondent, and they had only a stereotyped letter of explanation to guide them. Once completed, the respondents were asked to post back the pre-paid form. Research into social survey methods has shown time and again that non-responders to postal questionnaire surveys include a disproportionate number of the elderly, the less well-educated and the poor. The national survey of handicapped people had shown them to be concentrated among the elderly, who had grown up in an era of poor educational facilities, and those with low incomes[12] – in other words, among the social groups characterized by a poor response to postal surveys.

It is not surprising, therefore, that house-to-house inquiries were found to under-represent the total numbers of disabled people in an area, compared with the proportions revealed in the national survey and in well-conducted local sample surveys. Apart from this serious defect in most of the house-to-house inquiries, there was also the problem of keeping up to date any register of disabled people compiled on such a basis. After all, it was never expected that every impaired person identified by house-to-house inquiries would be found to need or to want a service which would keep him or her in contact with the social services department, thus facilitating a regular up-dating of records. Large numbers were anticipated to be managing satisfactorily for the present, and there was no provision for keeping up to date the register entries for these people. Over time, however, their circumstances might, and probably would, change – dependence might increase, a caring relative might fall ill, a supportive daughter might leave home – and a need for service arise. The fact that a person had once been registered but had been found to have no immediate need for any service would be of no assistance in providing a service promptly when need occurred if the register were out of date in respect of relevant circumstances.

The difficulty of up-dating records was mentioned in the circular sent to local authorities in September 1971, when those contemplating comprehensive individual identification were advised that the list of disabled people and their addresses would need to be continually revised, together with information about individual and family needs. This was a sensible warning, although it is doubtful if it was realized fully at the time how quickly and to what extent lists of disabled individuals would become out of date. Evidence of the speed and range of changes in the circumstances of disabled people has only recently become available.

One local authority area which had attempted a house-to-house identification of its disabled population subsequently permitted independent researchers to carry out a follow-up study of every handicapped individual under retirement age listed in the house-to-house enumeration.[13] Eighteen months elapsed between the completion of the house-to-house visits and the commencement of the interviewing programme for the second-stage survey. The household census was known to have led to an under-representation of those who were mentally handicapped and those with sensory defects, among whom the numbers identified were lower than those already recorded on existing local authority registers. None the less, the census had identified 1619 physically disabled people under retirement age (65 years for a man, 60 years for a woman) living in private households. This was the category on which the follow-up study concentrated. Every one of the 1619 names and addresses was included on the interview programme, but 465 of them were found to be beyond the scope of the second-stage survey. The reasons for this 'loss', in a period of only 18 months, of a third of those identified as younger disabled people are set out in table 2.

TABLE II *Persons found to be out of scope of the second-stage survey*

Reason for being beyond the scope	Nos. beyond scope of survey	% of all those beyond scope of survey
Over retirement age	148	32
Moved to unknown address or out of area	129	29
Dead	67	14
Mental handicap only	41	9
No permanent disability	33	7
Entered residential care	20	4
Other reasons (e.g. duplicate entry, non-existent address)	25	5
	463	100

It is true that the major factor that contributed to the 'loss' of disabled individuals who had previously been identified as under retirement age was simply that in the interval between the house-to-house census and the interview programme a number had reached that age. Whether or not disabled individuals are of retirement age is however, a material item of information for any register of disabled people that is compiled in order to facilitate the provision of services, because retirement marks a significant change in lifestyle for most people.

Moreover, our social security system, and certain special benefits for disabled people, such as the mobility allowance, are geared to a distinction between those who are, and those who are not, retirement pensioners.

A second large group lost in the 18-month interval comprised those who had moved. Some 60 of those who had moved house could be traced to their new address within the city boundary and were still included in the second-stage survey, but there remained 129 people who had moved away and could not be traced. It later became clear from the replies of respondents who completed the second-stage survey that disabled people generally are quite likely to move house in search of more convenient accommodation. Of the successfully interviewed population of 1095, 19 per cent had moved home at some time for reasons connected with their disablement. It is possible, given the fact that the initial house-to-house census that formed the basis for this survey was biased towards locomotor disablements, that this degree of household mobility was greater than would be found in a disabled population that fully represented people disabled by sensory or mental handicaps. None the less, the evidence is that disabled people are far from static, and any register of them would need to make provision for up-dating addresses quite frequently if it were to remain of use.

If we exclude altogether the entries that were incorrect at the time of the house-to-house enumeration, on the grounds that these mistakes cannot properly be regarded as indicating a need for regular up-dating, it still appears that 364, or nearly a quarter, of the people listed as physically disabled, under retirement age and living in private households had experienced a significant change in their circumstances in a period of 18 months – and this is in addition to those who had moved house but were successfully traced to their new addresses. Even this does not provide a complete picture of all the relevant changes that occurred, since the study gave no information on, for example, those disabled people whose physical condition had worsened or perhaps improved. Nor was there any information on those who had suffered a bereavement during the 18 months, those in whose families children had been born or those whose children had left home and were no longer providing support. All these circumstances require adjustment and are likely to cause some stress in normal households. In families already burdened by disablement, such changes may well precipitate a crisis.

Further evidence of the substantial changes in circumstances that can affect disabled individuals over a short space of time comes from the work of the University of Kent Health Services Research Unit.[14] Some 1608 physically impaired persons were identified by a survey of every household in Canterbury. A little over two years later a follow-up study revealed that over a quarter of all the disabled people identified had died, had gone into hospital or residential care permanently, or had moved out of the district. In addition, over half of those remaining in the survey had experienced some deterioration in their condition, resulting in a reduced capacity for independent living. The research team concluded:

> It is only the minority of people with handicaps who have a physical impairment resulting in a situation which is static over many years .... Changes in the capabilities of the people followed up were reflected in changes in their needs for aids, gadgets, adaptations and other help from statutory and voluntary services.[15]

There is at present, however, no proven way of keeping a register of disabled people in a manner that will alert responsible authorities when there is a change in an individual's circumstances that might indicate a need for supporting services. It is known that a number of emergency admissions of disabled people are a consequence of breakdowns in domestic arrangements.[16] The ability to identify those at risk − those who, although they were coping satisfactorily without supporting services, were vulnerable to deteriorating change in circumstances − would perhaps enable help to be offered promptly when need arose, thus reducing emergency admissions, which can so often lead to permanent institutional placements.

For this purpose, social services departments would need a reliable list of the names and addresses of every substantially impaired person, kept routinely up-dated whether the disabled person were in receipt of supporting services or not, together with information about changed circumstances which bore on the individual's capacity to cope or to obtain assistance. Clearly, the organization of such an information system would be time-consuming and expensive and might be resisted by some disabled persons as an invasion of their privacy. In any case, at the time when local authorities were being asked to compile registers of their disabled populations, they did not command the type of service that could provide, even for a short period, the sort of personal care that might be needed by a handicapped person at any hour of any day or night of the week and that should be available in order to avert emergency admissions in the way suggested above. It is understandable, therefore, that enthusiasm for individual identification of disabled people waned quite rapidly and that it was not revived when the Labour Government came to power and the chief architect of Section 1, Alf Morris, became Minister for the Disabled.

New incentives to register disabled persons

In recent years there has been a growth of personal care services for disabled people living at home. The first of these schemes known as Crossroads, was based on Rugby. It was quite small in scope and was financed partly by a grant from a television company that produced a programme of the same name in which one of the characters was depicted as physically handicapped. The success of this venture in giving regular respite to overburdened relatives and providing short-term emergency substitute care led to the development of similar schemes in other areas. A further stimulus to the provision of personal care services was the availability, after 1976, of funds that were at the disposal of an area health authority for expenditure on projects agreed jointly with its corresponding local authority to improve services, particularly for the elderly and the handicapped. In several areas this joint funding has been directed towards the development of some form of domiciliary personal care that is neither nursing care nor domestic help, but something of both, and that can be made available to handicapped people in order to give relatives a rest, or to avoid or postpone institutional admission. The exact nature of the service available differs from area to area, and the coverage of the country under such schemes as are currently in operation is very small. By no means all the personal care services are able to offer assistance to any handicapped person in their areas of operation, irrespective of his or her age, handicap or household composition, at any hour of the day or night, any day of the week, when such help might be required. Some of them do offer this sort of flexible service, however, which provides over-stressed relatives with the relief that enables them to continue giving care to a heavily dependent family member or offers a real alternative to institutional admission for a disabled person with no family to care for him or her or whose care arrangements have temporarily broken down.

With the increasing availability of this sort of service, there is an incentive for local authorities to look again at the possibility of identifying at least the most dependent of their handicapped citizens and attempting to keep their records up to date in order to anticipate and avert institutional admission by supplying assistance promptly at the time and in the form needed.

Any such register of disabled individuals in vulnerable circumstances is unlikely to be compiled on the basis of a mass exercise, such as was envisaged in Section 1 of the 1970 Act. Most of the personal care services currently operating have not relied on local authority registers of disabled people to find their clients, but have built up their own records and case loads on the basis of referrals from social workers, district nurses, general practitioners and disabled persons themselves or their friends or relatives. Already opportunities are appearing for the pooling of information about very vulnerable individuals and their families between community nursing services, social work services, doctors and the organizers of personal care services – a hopeful prospect for the development of an effective system of identifying the needs of very dependent disabled people.

None of the services for handicapped individuals is conditional upon the recipient's being first recorded on a local authority register. Neither is the entry of a person's name on the register any guarantee that he or she will receive any service at all. It is true that more of those who are registered are in receipt of services than those who are not registered, but this is chiefly because application and receipt of a service identifies a person as handicapped and his or her case is then recorded. In other words, it is the fact that a service has been asked for and given that leads to entry on the register for many disabled people, rather than the other way round.

There is certainly still a good deal of ignorance on the part of disabled people about services provided by the local authority for which they may be eligible, but merely registering a person as disabled does little or nothing to broaden his knowledge of services that could assist him. The dissemination of information to disabled people about services can be, and usually is quite independent of any register.

There does not seem, therefore, any need to regret the somewhat half-hearted way in which Section 1 of the Chronically Sick and Disabled Persons Act was implemented. Nor is there anything really significant, from the point of view of the welfare of disabled people, in the fact that by 1976 the number of names of disabled people entered on local authority registers, happened to approximate, as Alf Morris pointed out, to the estimate of 1,200,000 appreciably or severely handicapped people made in the national survey carried out by the Office of Population Censuses and Surveys. The registers were out of date and virtually useless.

Almost before the Act had reached the Statute Book, it became apparent that the chief reason for the failure of handicapped people to benefit from supporting services was that not enough resources were devoted to providing an adequate and appropriate range of support. Nor was there any prospect of the massive redirection or increase of resources necessary to expand services and facilities if help were to be given to all households with a handicapped member who wished for assistance.

Section 1 reflected the assumption that provided the presumably small number of really needy disabled people could be identified, a major improvement in their lives could be effected by a relatively minor increase in expenditure and effort. Once this assumption was abandoned in the light of the information produced by the national survey, which revealed the large numbers and many needs of handicapped people, Section 1 ceased to have any real meaning in the fight to obtain improvements in the welfare of disabled people. Resources, not registration, were the first priority.

NOTES

1. *H. C. Deb.*, vol. 722, col. *196*
2. *H. C. Deb.*, vol. 730, col. 1213; and H. C. Deb., vol. 741, col.69.

3. *Report of the Committee on Local Authority and Allied Personal Social Services* (the Seebohm Report), Cmnd 3703, HMSO, London, 1968.
4. DHSS Circular 12/70, 17 August 1970, para. 5.
5. A Harris, *Handicapped and Impaired in Great Britain,* HMSO, London, 1971; J. Buckle *Work and Housing of Impaired Persons in Great Britain,* HMSO, London, 1971.
6. *H. C. Deb.,* vol. 813, cols. 1160 – 1.
7. Harris, *Handicapped and Impaired in Great Britain.*
8. DHSS Circular 45/71, 16 September 1971.
9. The Chronically Sick and Disabled Persons Act, 1970, Section 1 (1).
10. *H. C. Deb.,* vol. 914, col. *661*
11. Report by the Department of Social Administration, Birmingham University, 1976.
12. A. Harris, C. R. W. Smith and E. Head, *Income and Entitlement to Supplementary Benefit of Impaired People in Great Britain*, HMSO, London, 1972.
13. The follow-up study was carried out by E. P. Topliss, with a grant from the Social Science Research Council and assistance from the local authority concerned, Southampton County Borough. A report of the study is lodged with the Social Science Research Council, and many of the findings are incorporated in E. Topliss, *Provision for the Disabled*, 2nd edn., Basil Blackwell and Martin Robertson, Oxford and London, 1979.
14. M. D. Warren, Rose Knight, and J. L. Warren, *Changing Capabilities and Needs of People with Handicaps,* Health Services Research Unit Report No.39, University of Kent, Canterbury, 1979.
15. ibid., p. 69.
16. J. Marks, *Young Physically Disabled Dependents and their Families,* Rehabilitation Department, Southampton General Hospital, 1977.

CHAPTER EIGHT

Improving Welfare Services for Disabled People

The emphasis of the Chronically Sick and Disabled Persons Act 1970 was on the disabled person living in a private household. This is understandable, because the vast majority of disabled people do live in ordinary households. It also reflected the view, which was being increasingly (and somewhat uncritically) accepted in the 1960s, that institutional care was intrinsically in almost all circumstances less satisfactory than living at home, for every individual who did not need elaborate hospital therapy.

The Act therefore concerned itself very little with residential facilities, and concentrated instead on the provision of welfare services for disabled people living in their own homes. Section 1 of the Act imposed a duty on each local authority to discover how many such people there were in its area, and to inform them of the services available to them. Section 2 specified the services which local authorities were required to provide for those of their disabled and chronically ill citizens who needed them.

As Chapter Six has indicated, local authorities were making some welfare provisions for disabled people even before the Act, but the coverage was very uneven and inequitable between one part of the country and another. The assumption of many who supported Alf Morris's Act was that some local authorities were evading their moral duty to their disabled population by refraining from exercising the powers to provide welfare services to handicapped individuals that had been conferred on them under Section 29 of the National Assistance Act 1948.

Consequently, Section 2 of the Chronically Sick and Disabled Persons Act imposed a duty on all local authorities to provide a specified range of supporting services for any of their disabled citizens in need of them. The survey of impaired people in Britain that was being conducted by the Office of Population Censuses and Surveys at the time when Alf Morris was preparing his Bill collected information on such matters as whether the impaired person had a television, a radio, a telephone, opportunities for leisure activities and holidays, and help in the house. These are the facilities that Alf Morris sought to ensure for all handicapped people who could benefit from them, and the services that Section 2 made mandatory are as follows:

1 Practical assistance for disabled people in their own homes.
2 Assistance for those who could not otherwise afford them to obtain radio and television facilities, and help to obtain library or similar recreational facilities in disabled persons' own homes.
3 Provision of similar recreational facilities outside their homes and assistance with use of educational facilities.
4 Provision of travel facilities to facilitate participation in such recreational, educational or other similar facilities.
5 Assistance with home adaptations and the provision of additional facilities to secure the greater comfort, safety or convenience of disabled persons at home.
6 Assistance in taking holidays.
7 Provision of meals, either in the home or elsewhere.
8 Assistance in obtaining telephones and any necessary special equipment for use by disabled persons.

Continuing variability of provision

The Act was therefore quite specific about the type and range of services to assist disabled people that local authorities had a duty to provide. Whatever hopes there may have been in 1970 that this would eliminate the unacceptably wide differences in provision between one authority and another must have been badly shaken by the evidence on continuing inequities.

Table 3, based on DHSS statistics for local authority personal social services for the twelve months from April 1st 1977 to March 31st 1978, shows how great a gap still existed between the most helpful and the most niggardly local authorities in respect of each of a number of services for disabled people. Cuts in social services budgets since 1978 have ensured that the low-spending authorities could not thereafter close the gap even if they had wished to do so.

TABLE III   *Variations between authorities in provision of specified services**

Service	Average all England	Highest provider	Lowest provider
Practical assistance – home help service†	90.8 clients	193.6 clients	37.8 clients
Adaptations			
private property	0.7	8.3	0.0
local authority	0.7	3.8	0.0
Personal aids	4.7	17.9	1.0
Radio & TV	0.9	63.0	0.0
Telephone & attachments	2.1	18.3	0.3

*Numbers helped expressed as a rate per 1000 of the population in the relevant area.

†In the case of the home help service, the figures indicate the number of clients over 65 (among whom will be many handicapped persons) as a rate per 1000 of the population over 65 in the relevant area.

Some local authorities were at the top end of provision across a whole range of services, while other local authorities were as consistently near the bottom end of provision of most services for disabled people. Unfortunately, it is not possible to be sure that these differences in the general level of performance in respect of help to disabled people have persisted over time, because local authority statistics have not been kept in such a way as to permit comparison across the range of services over the years. It is only possible to look at earlier performances in respect of the home help service and residential care provision for elderly people, among whom are found many of the chronically sick and disabled. As far as these two areas of provision are concerned, it appears from table 4 (based on DHSS statistics for local authority personal social services for 1974–75 and 1977–78) that the low performers

TABLE IV *Consistency of high or low performance by local authorities across a range of services for disabled people*

Authority	Service*					
	Telephone	Aids	Adaptations LA	Private	Home help†	Residential care**
Low performers						
Buckinghamshire	1.7	2.0	0.0	0.0	68.9 (61.7)	14.2 (15.3)
Cambridgeshire	0.1	2.9	0.1	0.2	74.3 (60.6)	13.9 (16.3)
Lincolnshire	0.4	4.5	0.1	0.1	78.3 (73.6)	17.2 (**)
High performers						
Oldham	3.2	10.5	1.1	0.9	161.5(149.5)	20.8 (21.9)
Camden	9.8	8.1	1.6	0.8	124.9(131.8)	32.8 (24.9)
Hammersmith	4.2	6.7	1.4	1.0	92.2 (92.9)	24.6 (22.6)
Islington	18.3	9.8	2.4	0.7	127.4(116.0)	30.0 (25.1)
Lambeth	5.6	5.7	2.2	1.5	124.5(120.3)	24.0 (29.4)
Lewisham	10.9	6.9	2.7	1.7	149.2(137.9)	20.2 (24.7)
Tower Hamlets	3.8	7.1	2.9	0.2	135.7(146.5)	27.2 (28.1)
Wandsworth	14.5	17.9	3.4	2.0	127.4(114.4)	21.8 (30.7)
All England	2.1	4.7	0.7	0.7	90.8 (82.5)	17.5 (17.3)

*Numbers expressed as a rate per 1000 of the population in the relevant area.

†In the case of the home help service and residential care, the figures indicate the number of recipients over 65 (among whom will be many chronically sick and handicapped persons) as a rate per 1000 of the population over 65 in the relevant area.

**There were no figures for residential care for the county of Lincolnshire as a whole for 1974−75.

among local authorities in 1977–78 were low performers in 1974–75, and had not brought the level of their services nearer to that of the better authorities in the intervening years. The rates for 1974–75 are given in brackets.

The inescapable conclusion is that notwithstanding the obligatory and specific duties imposed on local authorities by Section 2 of the Chronically Sick and Disabled Persons Act 1970, great differences in provision by local authorities continued. Furthermore, it is apparent from Table 4 that even some of the high performers among local authorities were, in 1977–78, providing a Home Help service, or residential care facilities, or both, at a lower rate per 1000 of the relevant population than was the case in 1974–75. Any increases in provision which they may have made must have been more than swallowed up by the increase in numbers of their elderly populations.

Increased provision and increased need

There is a general problem of relating the increased expenditure in real terms, made by local authorities as a whole on services for disabled people, to the increase in need which took place over the same period. Some of the increase in need was a consequence of the growth in the numbers of elderly people, among whom many disabling conditions are to be found. In addition, however, the emphasis placed by Section 1 of the Chronically Sick and Disabled Persons Act on identifying the numbers of disabled people in the population meant that the numbers of people known to be handicapped and likely to require supporting services increased as fast as, or faster than, the provision of services. Consequently, the proportion of people known to be disabled who received assistance from local authority services probably did not increase much, if at all. Neither, it seems likely, has the average level of help to each disabled recipient increased significantly since the passing of the Act.

None the less, there is no doubt at all that there has been an increase in the numbers of people receiving some assistance from local authorities in respect of needs created by disability. The numbers of households with a disabled member receiving some assistance under Section 2 increased by almost 60 per cent between

1972 and 1978. It is true that the initial base from which the development of services has been measured was extremely small at the beginning of the 1970s, so that even quite minor increases in provision show as large percentage improvements. This is the likely explanation for the fact that the percentage rate of growth in local authority welfare provision for disabled citizens was higher in the first half of the decade than in the second, although for the latter period Alf Morris, the architect of the Chronically Sick and Disabled Persons Act, was at the DHSS as Minister with special responsibility for the welfare of disabled people, and he gave energetic encouragement to the development of services by local authorities, at least in the early period of his office. By the end of the 1970s the cuts in local authority budgets curbed all growth in services and in some cases led to actual reductions in provision. As the numbers of elderly and disabled people were still increasing at the time of the economic cuts even a standstill in the availability of supporting services represented a greater number of handicapped people experiencing neglect.

It is also pertinent to note that during the period in which the number of people receiving local authority services under Section 2 had increased by 60 per cent, the numbers of handicapped persons entered on local authority registers increased by 100 per cent, so that the expansion of services did not permit the maintenance of the same level of help to all people discovered to be disabled as had been available to the smaller number previously identified.

It is possible, of course, that the more severely disabled people would have come to the notice of the local authority soonest and would therefore have been among those registered earliest. Later additions to the register would then have included a higher proportion of less severely disabled people who might not have required services. There is some evidence that the majority of disabled individuals who receive no welfare services do not want to make use of any of the local authority services currently available.[1] If this is the case, the 60 per cent increase in provision of services should mean that there has been a real reduction in unsatisfied demand among disabled people, despite the increased number of handicapped individuals now known to be living in the community. This was indeed the picture revealed in a study carried out in one local authority area, which showed that between 1971, when the Act first began to be implemented, and 1974 there had been a marked reduction in unsatisfied demand for services among both those known to be disabled in 1971 and those who became classified as handicapped at a later date.[2]

One could therefore be cautiously optimistic about the extent to which the increased provision of local authority services since 1970 has represented a real contribution to the welfare of a greater percentage of handicapped people. At the same time, there seem to be no grounds for complacency, since the evidence suggests that even before the economic cuts of 1979 – 80, unsatisfied demand persisted for such basic assistance as the provision of rails round the WC or bath, for telephones, holidays and library facilities. Above all, there remained considerable inequity of provision according to the local authority area in which a disabled person happened to live.

Problems of enforcing the provisions of the Act

Quite soon after the Chronically Sick and Disabled Persons Act reached the Statute Book, some unease began to be expressed about the way in which local authorities were implementing, or failing to implement, Section 2. Hansard records a number of questions asked on this topic in the House of Commons during the Session in 1971 – 72. The replies to these questions by spokesmen for the Conservative Government returned in the election held immediately after the Act was passed were bland and evasive. Some early questioners were told that it was too soon to assess the response of local authorities to the Act.[3] Notwithstanding this lack of information, a question asked by Alf Morris very little later about the performance of local authorities in respect of Section 2 received the confident assurance that 'all local authorities are implementing this Section.'[4] No details were given, and Alf Morris's subsequent request that the DHSS should call for returns from local authorities showing how they were implementing Section 2 was refused.[5]

In fact, statistics have been collected by the DHSS on local authority personal social services, and those relating to the provisions of the Chronically Sick and Disabled Persons Act appeared for the first time for the 12 month period from April 1st 1972 to March 31st 1973. The form in which information has been collected and presented has varied over the years, making comparisons and the detection of trends difficult, if not impossible. Some areas of provision, such as leisure opportunities and transport facilities for disabled people, are not documented at all in the statistics available, and the figures given of numbers of people assisted with holidays do not permit the identification of handicapped beneficiaries. As has been agreed above, however, the somewhat unsatisfactory data that are available make it clear that no local authority is satisfying all the need expressed by the disabled population, and some authorities are doing much less than others in this respect.

Since the Chronically Sick and Disabled Persons Act 1970 was expressly framed to make it mandatory for local authorities to provide certain specified services for disabled people who needed them, it both puzzled and disappointed many people to find that uneven provision and unsatisfied demand for services persisted. How could local authorities evade their statutory obligations, apparently with impunity? This was the question that was asked more and more insistently by disappointed disabled people and by those concerned for their wellbeing.

Unfortunately, the Act carried no provisions for enforcement, so that even if the central Government had the will to secure the full implementation of the Act, it was not clear what, if anything, could be done about recalcitrant authorities. In any case, the largely uninformative and unhelpful replies that Conservative Government spokemen gave to questions about implementation during their period of office from 1970 until 1974 throws considerable doubt on their enthusiasm for coercing niggardly authorities into greater expenditure on services for disabled people.

In 1974, however, a Labour Government was returned, and Alf Morris was appointed the country's first Minister of State with special responsibility for the welfare of disabled people. His appointment held out the hope of a more energetic approach by central Government to the problem of ensuring that the provisions of the Act were implemented by local authorities. This hope was fostered by the fact that the Queen's Speech at the opening of the new Parliament, referred to the Government's intention to bring in further measures for the benefit of disabled people. There was a mood of renewed optimism among organizations of and for disabled people about governmental intention to ensure the full implementation of the Chronically Sick and Disabled Persons Act.

Quite early in the new parliamentary session the Minister for the Disabled said, in answer to a question about how policies for community care were reflecting the large increases in the numbers of disabled people on local authority registers: 'It is my policy systematically to build up services,' but he added, 'as resources permit'.[6]

This could only be interpreted as a clear indication that the duty imposed on local authorities by the Act to provide services for disabled people was not absolute but conditional upon the availability of resources. This interpretation appeared to be confirmed by a later statement made in the House by Alf Morris about the implementation of Section 2 of the Act, when he said:

> Our legal advice is that once a local authority accepts that need exists
> in respect of one of the services listed in that Section, it is incumbent
> on it to make arrangements to meet that need. In the present
> economic situation there are, of course, difficulties about balancing
> the discharge of the duty with due exercise of financial restraint.[7]

No such caveat about the availability of resources was mentioned by the Parliamentary Commissioner for Health and Social Services, Sir Idwal Pugh, when, later in the same year, he investigated a complaint by the father of a disabled girl whose local authority was not providing her with services under Section 2 of the Act and of which she was in need. The Ombudsman commented that legal advice sought by the DHSS had confirmed that a local authority could not plead lack of money as a reason for not meeting need.[8]

Once again, there was a small upsurge of confidence among disabled people that at last niggardly local authorities would be compelled to discharge their duties under Section 2. The later years of the decade 1970 – 80 showed this confidence to be unfounded. Despite the Ombudsman's unequivocal statement, local authorities continued to fail to meet a number of requests by disabled people for services under Section 2, and there was no obvious legal remedy open to a handicapped individual thus denied as long as the local authority concerned avoided acknowledging that he or she had a need for the service in question.

The Chronically Sick and Disabled Persons Act 1970 is ambiguously worded in a number of places. The haste with which the measure was drafted and private Members' general lack of expertise in such matters when framing their Bills may account for some of the ambiguities. On the other hand, it is also clear from the records of meetings of the *ad hoc* group formed to assist Alf Morris in the development of the Bill[9] that some wording was deliberately imprecise in order to avoid disputes and delays that might prove fatal to the passage of the Bill through both Houses of Parliament in the limited time available for private Members' measures.

This was certainly the case in respect of the terms 'chronically sick' and 'disabled' and 'chronic sickness' and 'disability'; some members of the *ad hoc* group who favoured giving precise definitions to the terms were persuaded that to attempt to do so would almost certainly delay the Bill and cause it to be lost. The concept of need was likewise recognized to be susceptible of differing interpretations, but no definition was attempted, and the determination of need was left to local authorities. Doubtless, a degree of ambiguity was necessary in order to facilitate the Bill's passage into law, but it has meant that the Statute thus established has been largely unenforceable.

In respect of Section 2, not only is there no precise definition of who is to be regarded as chronically sick or disabled, but there is no definition either of what constitutes a need for a service. Consequently, the legal advice that a local authority could not plead lack of resources as a reason for not meeting need only warned local authorities to be extremely careful not to admit need on the part of any disabled persons unless they were in a position readily to provide the necessary specified service or facility. Refusal on the part of a local authority to recognize a need expressed by a handicapped person had not, up to the end of the first decade of the operation of the Chronically Sick and Disabled Persons Act, been challenged in any way; nor is it easy to see the constitutional channels for making such a challenge.

The World Health Organization, when considering public health programmes in 1971, recognized that need is a relative concept, but suggested that it was useful to distinguish between *perceived* need as expressed by the individual concerned and *assessed* need as defined by the relevant professional.[10] It would be possible to apply this measurement of need to handicapped people and to use *assessed* need, rather than *perceived* need, as the criterion for determining whether a need existed that there was a statutory obligation on the local authority to meet. However, the relevant professionals involved in the assessments, such as social workers or occupational therapists, would need to be independent of the local authority concerned in order that the professional definition of need was not coloured by financial or political pressures.

It may be argued that even the eminently worthy aim of improving services for disabled people must be tempered by an understanding of practicalities, and that lack of resources simply must be a factor in any discussions about whether to make a service available at all, or available to a particular individual in particular circumstances at a particular time. Two points must be made in this connection. One is that the avoidable social disadvantages suffered by disabled people as a result of the social neglect of their needs over past years has meant that they often lack the opportunity to make their views clearly heard in discussions about priorities in the allocation of resources. The second point is that the evidence of considerable disparities between local authorities in the matter of help provided for disabled people shows that constraints on resources, which affect all of them alike, have been dealt with very differently by the different authorities. This is because moral choices, attitudes and values are involved in deciding priorities, as well as (perhaps as much as) practical exigencies.

Residential care

Although, as was mentioned at the beginning of this chapter, the Chronically Sick and Disabled Persons Act did not involve itself greatly with the provision of residential care for disabled people, there was in Sections 17 and 18 an expression of concern that many younger disabled people were being placed in accommodation that was really intended for the care of the very old. When Alf Morris had been preparing his Bill he received a number of letters from the public, several of which referred to the misery of young disabled people known or related to the writers, who were incarcerated in totally unsuitable residential accommodation, surrounded by very frail and senile old people, with whom the handicapped persons had nothing in common and could enjoy no companionship. It was impossible to know how general this predicament was for disabled people in residential accommodation, as there were no reliable statistics for younger handicapped people supported by local authorities in residential care.

The responsibility for providing residential accommodation for those who needed it by virtue of age or infirmity was imposed on local welfare authorities by the National Assistance Act 1948, and the Chronically Sick and Disabled Persons Act did nothing to modify this responsibility. It merely sought, in Sections 17 and 18, to oblige health and welfare authorities to provide information about the number of handicapped people under the age of 65 who were accommodated with elderly persons. These Sections instructed the Secretary of State at the DHSS to obtain such information from local authorities as he might require about the residential care of younger handicapped people, and to make such information annually available to Parliament in such form as he deemed appropriate.

Since 1970 the DHSS has regularly collected from local authorities a range of information about numbers and types of residential facilities, and numbers, ages and reasons for admission of the people in the units. Not until the returns of 1974–75, however, was this information available in the DHSS Personal Social Services Local Authority Statistics series on residential accommodation in a form that could throw much light on the circumstances of younger handicapped people in residential care. During 1974–75 there were some 7344 residents under the age of 65 supported by authorities in residential units with people over that age. This represented a decrease of 11.8 per cent since such statistics began to be collected in 1972.

Half of those under 65 who were accommodated with elderly people were themselves aged between 60 and 64. Some of these may have been prematurely senile and therefore appropriately placed in a home for elderly people. In most cases, however, the mere fact that a handicapped person was close to his or her 65th birthday was not a satisfactory reason for offering residential care, when needed, in a unit which was geared primarily to the needs of frail and senile old people, most of whom would be very much older than 65.

Less than one-fifth of handicapped people under 65 who were in residential accommodation with elderly people were younger than 50 and most of those were in special units for handicapped people run by voluntary organizations, such as the Leonard Cheshire Foundation. These units offer a home for life to those who enter, which inevitably means that some will reach and pass their 65th birthday while they are in the unit, though the majority of people there will be younger. Such a mix of ages is not unacceptable.

Fuller information about ages of people in residential care available for the period 1974 – 75 suggests, as the above comments should make plain, that merely knowing how many disabled people under 65 are accommodated in units with people over that age, and how many of these are themselves nearly 65, tells us little about whether or not the accommodation is suitable.

Current issues in residential care

After 1975 the statistics for residential accommodation do not show as great a preoccupation with the ages of residents. This is not a matter for regret, as has been argued above. It would be unfortunate, however, if, with the dropping of the issue, it was assumed that all handicapped persons in residential care were appropriately accommodated – or even that all those in need of such care could be sure of obtaining it.

As has already been pointed out, the obligation to provide residential accommodation for disabled people in need of it was imposed on local authorities by the National Assistance Act, 1948. While the architects of the Chronically Sick and Disabled Persons Act clearly suspected that this duty was not always discharged in the most satisfactory manner, their measure reflected no doubts that residential provision of some sort was made available when needed. This assumption was questionable in 1970 and certainly unfounded in the climate of the economic cuts of 1980.

Some very severely disabled people, unable any longer to cope with life in a private household, have reluctantly sought admission to residential care only to find either that a place is not available in a local authority unit, or that an offer of accommodation in a voluntary organization cannot be made until the local authority undertakes to accept financial responsibility for the costs of such care. In the period of tight budgetary restrictions at the end of the 1970s local authorities tended to restrict their sponsorship of disabled people in residential care by accepting no new cases until an existing responsibility expired. This form of economy was open to them because although local authorities had a duty to provide residential care for disabled people who needed it, once again there was no definition of need in the National Assistance Act 1948. Authorities were within their rights, therefore, to recognize only such need for residential care as was consistent with the resources they had allocated for the purpose. Need in excess of this amount, like that of the individuals whose stories are told below, went unacknowledged and unmet.

Mr S. had a promising executive career, a wife and two young sons when multiple sclerosis was diagnosed. As the disease progressed, it not only crippled him physically, but it also affected his personality, making him unreasonably demanding. His wife cared for him devotedly, despite the growing difficulties and stress, but finally she broke down and was admitted to hospital for treatment. The two boys were also reported by their school teachers to be showing signs of disturbance as a result of their difficult home conditions, which were jeopardizing their school careers. Mrs S.'s mother, aged 83, left her own husband alone in their home in the north of England to take care of her son-in-law and grandsons while her daughter was in hospital. A residential placement for Mr S. would have provided him with the attention he needed, enabled his wife and sons to lead a more normal life and freed his mother-in-law from a burden quite unreasonable for an 83-year-old person, allowing her to return to peaceful retirement with her husband. But no residential placement was available for Mr S., not was any hope at all held out to the family. The only solution in their unbearable position seemed to be to send the boys to an aunt in Australia, and for their mother to move in with her parents, leaving her husband to become a crisis admission to a hospital bed.

Mr P. was a teacher until Parkinson's Disease forced early retirement on him. His wife then took up a business appointment to keep the home going and to complete the education of their two sons. This meant Mr P. had to be left alone all day, and as the disease progressed he suffered frequent falls, several necessitating hospital admission. Finally, one fall resulted in a fractured leg, and two operations were necessary, after which Mr P was much more severely handicapped. His wife felt unable to keep him at home, where he would have to be left alone a good deal. The hospital was anxious to discharge Mr P., for whom it could do no more, and both he and his wife were continuously pressed to make other arrangements. The local authority made no offer of residential care, and after 18 months in hospital Mr P. entered a private nursing home, although his health insurance scheme would meet the very high fees for only 12 months and Mrs P. had sufficient savings, even with sale of their house and removal to a cheaper one, for a further year only. After that they did not know what would happen.

Miss W. was severely incapacitated with multiple sclerosis and lived with her elderly widowed mother, who suffered from arthritis. Miss W. was very conscious of the burden that she imposed on her mother and made as few demands as possible, never asking to be taken out or encouraging friends to visit. As an intelligent professional woman of 40, she found her narrow existence very depressing indeed. For her own sake as well as her mother's, she wanted a place in a residential care unit, but two years after applying she was still waiting, still worrying.

Situations like the three cited above are bound to become tragically common unless resources for residential care facilities for disabled people become more plentiful. At present, there is simply not enough provision to meet the desperate need of disabled people whose domestic arrangements have already broken down or are in imminent peril. In addition, there are many young disabled adults who are compelled to live at home with their parents because there is no constructive alternative that would offer them both the level of personal attention that they need and the chance to establish their own home, separate from their family of origin, that is the ambition of most young people.

Most residential care facilities, even those specially planned for younger disabled people, are based on collective living and dominated by an ethos of total care, which strips the resident of responsibility for his own life and decisions. Such conditions are unlikely to be appropriate for the vast majority of disabled people of any age, which is why residential care is sought as a last resort only when survival in a private household is threatened. For young people who still have the alternative of parental care, current conditions in most residential units hold out no hope of greater personal development and maturity than can be had at home.

The fact that there is little demand from young people for the type of residential care that is, for the most part, currently available for disabled people should not be taken to mean that their needs are satisfied; rather, it should be understood for what it really is − a protest against the inappropriateness of much of the existing provision of residential accommodation for disabled people. The principle of less eligibility which was used to justify harsh conditions in workhouses in order to deter the poor from seeking admission, has its modern expression in the way that residential care for disabled people is generally provided in less attractive form than any but the most completely unsatisfactory home conditions.

In the light of what has been said above, it seems reasonable to conclude, from our vantage point ten years after the passing of the Chronically Sick and Disabled Persons Act, that the emphasis in Sections 17 and 18 on the separation of people under 65 from those over 65 in residential care was misplaced. What is more, the implicit suggestion that there is a natural watershed between the ages of 64 and 65 is dangerously misleading. For administrative purposes such as the issuing of retirement pensions, old age has to be deemed to begin at a specific point in the life cycle that is standard for all people, but it is entirely unhelpful to use this administrative fiction to determine what is and what is not a suitable environment for a disabled person in need of residential accommodation. The real issues are the desperate shortage of facilities and the fact that standards and variety in the provision of residential accommodation are not commensurate with the expectations and variety of needs of disabled individuals.

The welfare services for disabled people with which the Chronically Sick and Disabled Persons Act was concerned expanded in the decade 1970 – 80. Some, like the home help service and residential facilities for elderly people, among whom are found many chronically sick and disabled individuals, increased at a rate that barely kept pace with the rate of increase in the numbers of elderly people – they had to run in order to stand still, as it were. Some, like the services to assist disabled people to obtain a telephone or a television or radio set, after an initial rise began to decrease towards the end of the 1970s, although (at least as far as telephones were concerned) demand from disabled people still persisted. On the other hand, assistance with telephone rental charges and television licence fees increased, indicating that local authority funds were increasingly being used to supplement the inadequate maintenance allowances paid to disabled people by central Government rather than to expand personal social services.

Unmet need for services, including residential accommodation, still exists ten years after the passing of the Act. Despite the mandatory nature of local authorities' obligation under Section 2 of the Chronically Sick and Disabled Persons Act, it has not proved possible to enforce full implementation, and much disparity of provision between authorities remains.

NOTES

1. See E. Topliss, *Provision for the Disabled*, 2nd edn., Basil Blackwell and Martin Robertson, Oxford and London, 1979, chapter nine, for a report of a survey of disabled people indicating that while only a third received any local authority services, three-quarters of those who did not receive services did not want any.
2. M. D. Warren, R. Knight and J. L. Warren, *Changing Capabilities and Needs of People with Handicaps*, Health Services Research Unit Report No. 39, University of Kent, Canterbury, 1979, pp. 47 – 50.
3. *H. C. Deb.*, vol. 805, col. *282*; and *H. C. Deb.*, vol. 811, col. *250*.
4. *H. C. Deb.*, vol. 815, col. *64*.
5. *H. C. Deb.*, vol. 816, col. *300 – 1*.
6. *H. C. Deb.*, vol. 882, col. *682*.
7. *H. C. Deb.*, vol. 904, cols. *235 – 6*.
8. *Sixth Report of the Parliamentary Commissioner for Administration 1975 – 76*, HC 665, HMSO, London 1976. Case No. C.12/K.
9. The author is indebted to the Rt. Hon. Alfred Morris, MP, for the use of his private records of meetings during the period of preparation of the Chronically Sick and Disabled Persons Bill.
10. World Health Organization, *Statistical Indicators for the Planning and Evaluation of Public Health Programmes*, Technical Report Series No. 472, WHO, Geneva, 1971.

CHAPTER NINE

Somewhere to Live and Somewhere to Go

After requiring local authorities to determine the numbers of their disabled citizens and to provide those in need of them with specific services, the main emphasis of the Chronically Sick and Disabled Persons Act was on improving housing and access facilities for disabled people.

Housing

It has already been noted that at the time Alf Morris was preparing his Bill, the Office of Population Censuses and Surveys was carrying out a survey on behalf of the Government to ascertain the numbers of handicapped people living in the community and to discover something about their circumstances. One aspect of the living conditions of disabled people studied in the survey was that of housing, and it was found that nearly one million impaired people in Britain needed rehousing or substantial improvements to their existing dwellings.[1] This represented the number of disabled people who were estimated to be living in accommodation without an indoor WC convenient for the use of the disabled, or who were obliged to sleep in a living-room, or who were unable to gain access to some of the rooms in their homes.

Alf Morris therefore included in his measure, in Section 3, the requirement that housing authorities should have regard to the housing needs of disabled people in planning future dwellings. They were also required, when making their annual returns to central Government showing the provision of new houses, to distinguish dwellings that were intended for the accommodation of disabled persons.

120

The entire thrust of Section 3 was towards the public housing sector, despite the fact that home ownership was increasing rapidly in popularity, and is now the form of tenure of over half the households in Britain. The emphasis on local authority housing in the Act was largely a matter of expediency, as assisting disabled people to obtain more suitable accommodation in the private housing market was beyond the scope of Alf Morris's private Member's Bill. There were also good reasons for believing that local authority housing could make a major contribution towards improving the living conditions of many disabled people.

The survey carried out by the Office of Population Censuses and Surveys had found that 29 per cent of their sample of impaired people were living in local authority dwellings, and nearly a third of these would have liked to move to a more convenient dwelling. A further 19 per cent of the impaired respondents were living in privately rented accommodation, and almost half of these people wanted to move for reasons connected with their disability. Even among the owner-occupiers, who accounted for a third of all the impaired people in the sample, 20 per cent found their houses unsuitable for their disabled condition and expressed a wish to move. Many of the owner-occupiers were elderly people living in older housing who did not have the financial resources to buy more convenient (and inevitably more expensive) properties, so they also were looking to the local authority as their best hope for rehousing.

The initial response of local authorities to Section 3 was slow — only 16 dwellings for disabled people were built in the 18 months after the Act was passed, and fewer proposals for these specially designed houses were submitted by local authorities in 1972 than had been the case in 1971. By the end of 1978 a total of 3122 local authority houses specially designed for wheelchair occupants had been built, and a further 1231 such houses were under construction.[2]

Local authority proposals for this type of housing reached a peak of 863 in 1975, the year after a general election had returned a Labour Government and Alf Morris had been appointed Minister with special responsibility for the welfare of disabled people. After 1975 the numbers of local authority proposals for wheelchair housing began to fall, but housing associations then began to play a bigger part in meeting the housing needs of handicapped people. By the end of 1978 housing associations had provided 303 specially designed houses or flats for disabled people, and had nearly 1000 more under construction.

The increasing role of housing associations in the provision of specialized accommodation for disabled people, and the reduction of local authority commitment to this type of provision, were both responses to a Department of Environment Circular 74/74, which was sent out to all local authorities a few months after Alf Morris had taken up his ministerial appointment. The circular began by asserting that there was an urgent need for housing authorities to do much more for people who were physically handicapped – 'and to help housing associations to do so too'. There then followed a summary of the characteristics of the majority of disabled people that were related to their housing needs, as revealed by the survey of impaired people carried out by the Office of Population Censuses and Surveys. Among the handicapped, the circular reminded housing authorities, 58 per cent were over 65, and a further 27 per cent were between 50 and 64. The majority of both these groups lived alone or in two-person households, which indicated that the main need was for one- or two-bedroomed accommodation, with only a small amount of accommodation needed for larger family units with a disabled member. Only 25 per cent of all adult disabled people were totally dependent on wheelchairs, but many others had limited mobility. The circular therefore advised, since the housing needs of disabled people were not all the same, that there should be a variety of provision. The circular suggested three approaches to meeting the housing needs of disabled people: to upgrade existing houses to standards suitable for the disabled occupant; to provide specially designed wheelchair housing; to provide ordinary housing with level access designed to a standard of space and amenity suitable for occupation by a disabled person, called 'mobility housing'.

The concept of mobility housing was a new one, and it marked offical recognition of the fact that housing specially designed for wheelchair occupants was neither needed nor wanted by the vast majority of disabled people. The obligation which Section 3 had placed on local authorities to distinguish housing designated for disabled people when making their returns to the Department of Environment had not included any requirement that the accommodation thus separately recorded should be of any particular design. In practice, however, if local authorities were to qualify for the special subsidies towards the cost of building houses for disabled people that were available from central Government, the design of the dwellings had to conform to certain standards. These standards included level access, accommodation all on one floor, wide doorways and expansive circulation space, and specially fitted kitchens and bathrooms. The image of the potential occupant was obviously that of a young wheelchair-bound adult with a small family – not by any means typical of the disabled population.

It is quite possible, therefore, to believe, as reported by Selwyn Goldsmith, superintending architect of the Housing Development Directorate of the Department of the Environment, that some local authorities had experienced difficulties in finding suitable tenants to occupy the wheelchair housing that they had built. Goldsmith concluded that there was less need for specially designed housing for disabled people than had been supposed and more need for the mobility housing that had been referred to in the Department of Environment Circular 74/74, which Goldsmith has described more fully.[3]

From his development of the concept of mobility housing, it is clear that the reasons for wanting to minimize reliance on specially designed housing for the accommodation of disabled people were logistically and economically sound and also humane. As has been said above, purpose-built family homes designed for wheelchair occupants did not reflect the housing needs of the majority of disabled people, and they were also expensive to build. Furthermore, as these specially designed units were usually constructed in small enclaves on the edges of ordinary housing developments, the occupants were often isolated. The limited number of such dwellings meant that a prospective tenant had to be prepared to go wherever the accommodation happened to be available, which sometimes involved moving a considerable distance from supporting relatives, friends and neighbours.

It therefore made good sense to look carefully at the design of ordinary public-sector housing to see how far this could meet the needs of most disabled people who required improved accommodation. In fact, however most local authority housing of recent years has been low-rise flats without lifts, or two-storey family houses with bedrooms and bathrooms on the upper floors and the principle living-rooms below. Apart from the flats on the ground floor of low-rise blocks, the above types of accommodation cannot offer disabled people the level entrance and accessibility to all rooms and facilities implied by the idea of mobility housing.

The standards required to qualify a dwelling as mobility housing were consequently revised and are now satisfied by both ground-floor flats and two-storey houses with the following features: an accessible entrance – no steps and a low threshold sill, and doorsets and passages at least 900 mm wide – which will just permit wheelchair transit; and (in the case of two-storey houses) level access to ground-floor rooms, a ground-floor WC, and a straight staircase to which a mechanical stairlift may be fitted if the disabled occupant needs one to gain access to the bedroom and bathroom.

This revision of mobility standards to include two-storey housing as described above meant that a considerable proportion of public-sector housing could be considered suitable for occupation by disabled people. Such accommodation would be part of ordinary housing developments and not segregated in any ways, and the fact that the dwellings of disabled people were no different in design from other neighbouring properties would make it easier for handicapped people to go visiting occasionally instead of being restricted to their own four walls.

Mobility housing of the above standard might have been expected to make a significant improvement to the accommodation of disabled people, one million of whom, it must be remembered, were believed to be in urgent need of housing more suited to their impaired capacities. The response of local authorities to Circular 74/74 in respect of mobility housing encouraged optimism. In the first full year after the circular was issued, local authorities began to construct 186 mobility housing units, and proposals for another 600 were in the pipeline. Housing associations were also encouraged to develop housing to mobility standards, and over 400 proposals were received from them in the first 12 months. Altogether over the four years 1975, 1976, 1977 and 1978 local authorities and housing associations between them completed over 5000 units of mobility housing and had 13500 more under construction.[4]

Clearly, mobility housing was a feasible, even popular proposition for local authorities as a means of meeting the housing needs of their disabled citizens, in a way wheelchair housing had never been. The commitment of local authorities to providing housing to mobility standards is indicated by the fact that although the subsidy from central Government attaching to such dwellings was fixed at £50 per unit in 1975 and had been increased to only £60 in 1978 – an increase that did not keep up with inflation and rising costs – there was no apparent reduction in local authority enthusiasm for mobility housing, which continued to increase.

This satisfactory situation came to an end with the curtailment of public-sector house building following the return of a Conservative Government in the election of 1979. Sheltered housing and housing specifically for disabled or elderly occupants were exempted from the requirements of the Housing Act 1980. Existing stocks of mobility and wheelchair housing will not therefore be depleted by sale to existing tenants and subsequently on the open market. On the other hand, further expansion of provision is unlikely while public sector housing generally is in decline. The shift of emphasis in housing policies since 1979 from public-sector housing to speculative development financed by private enterprise can only mean that there is now less chance that disabled people will find accommodation suited to their needs, since many are elderly, have lower-than-average incomes, and are not able to compete for property on the private market.[5]

Improvements and alterations to existing properties

With the decline in public-sector building, there is a greater need than ever to adapt and improve existing housing of disabled people. Section 2 of the Chronically Sick and Disabled Persons Act imposed a duty on local authority social services departments to assist disabled people to obtain adaptations to their housing. As we saw in Chapter Eight, the number of households assisted in this way increased after the passing of the Act, but as far as property other than council houses was concerned, nearly 90 per cent of the adaptations made under this provision were modifications costing less than £150 apiece. Clearly, only minor work could be carried out for this sum, and such alterations as installing a stairlift, constructing a downstairs WC or widening doorways could very seldom have been undertaken. Circular 74/74 had stressed up-grading existing houses as one important means of achieving appropriate standards of housing for disabled people, but local authority statistics show no great response to this suggestion.

In 1978 Department of Environment Circular 59/78 was sent to local authorities on the subject of adaptations to housing for people who were physically disabled. This circular emphasized that both housing authorities and social services departments had powers to adapt houses for the convenience and safety of disabled people, but that the overlapping responsibilities should not be allowed to cause confusion or delay in making necessary improvements. The circular therefore proposed that structural adaptations to private properties, such as the provision of ramps or handrails, the installation of an entryphone system or remote-control window openers, and the equipment of kitchens at wheelchair height, should be the responsibility of the housing department, which could claim a subsidy for such work done in order to make a dwelling suitable for a disabled occupant. The social services departments were to be responsible for assisting disabled people to obtain non-structural aids and for identifying and assessing needs for structural adaptations. The circular recognized that this was a considerable modification of Section 2 of the Chronically Sick and Disabled Persons Act, which charged local authority social services departments with responsibility for both adaptations to property and the provision of aids. The fact that the Chronically Sick and Disabled Persons Act imposed statutory responsibilities for adaptations on social services departments should not, the circular warned, be made an excuse for the failure of housing departments to use their powers to carry out modifications on properties of disabled people.

Circular 59/78 also made it clear that any structural modifications to property proposed in order to benefit a disabled person could legitimately be included in an application for an improvement grant, that is, a grant available to help meet the cost of work on privately owned or rented accommodation that was necessary in order to make the dwelling suitable for occupation by a disabled person.

Many improvements to property made in order to facilitate occupation by a disabled person are of a type that render the property liable for higher rates. Some disabled individuals successfully appealed against an increase in the rateable value of their properties arguing that the modification in question was not, for them, an improvement but a basic and essential amenity. Yet in many cases there was no doubt that the adaptation – the construction of a garage for example, or the addition of a downstairs bathroom – did constitute a real improvement to the property and ought properly to have attracted a higher rateable value. At the same time, disabled people with low incomes could be dissuaded from accepting financial help to make much needed adaptations for fear of the increased rate demand that would follow. In 1978 the Rating (Disabled Persons) Act was passed, which, after it came into effect in April 1979, meant that although any adaptations that constituted improvements to properties would be taken into account in fixing a new rateable value, rate relief would be available if the modification was essential for the safety or convenience of the disabled occupant.

It was clear that Circular 59/78 was trying to encourage greater use of existing powers under various pieces of past legislation in an effort to up-grade the existing housing of disabled people. The attempt was bound to be viewed with some scepticism, even without the cuts in public expenditure that occured after 1979 and affected the enthusiasm of both housing departments and social services departments for financing adaptations. The complications in the way of operating such complex and overlapping procedures were considerable.[6] There was far too much scope for buck-passing between the sections and departments involved, and in keeping an eye on the progress of the buck, it was only too easy to lose sight of the needs of the disabled individual.

Accessibility in the community

Although having somewhere safe and comfortable to live is of prior importance to disabled people, as it is to us all, the disabled also need to be able to leave their homes and enter into the life of the community. The Chronically Sick and Disabled Persons Act sought to promote the opportunities of disabled people to participate in such ordinary activities as shopping, transacting personal business at the bank, going to the theatre or having a drink in a pub, by improving accessibility in the community. Section 4 required that any new building to which the public would be admitted should make provision for the needs of disabled people, so far as it was both practicable and reasonable to do so. Sections 5 and 6 concerned the provision of toilet facilities by local authorities and in buildings open to the public, and these were to be designed having regard to the needs of disabled people, again so far as was both reasonable and practicable.

The inclusion of a waiver Clause in respect of the obligation to design buildings and facilities in accordance with the needs of disabled people was inevitable, given the general nature of the injunction, as otherwise a cafe opening at the top of an old martello tower to catch the beach tea trade, for example, could be required to install a lift and specially spacious and easily accessible lavatories for the use of customers whose wheelchairs could not anyway be pushed across soft sand or shingle beaches to get to the tower. None the less, however reasonable the inclusion of the waiver Clause, it has meant that the needs of disabled persons have continued to be disregarded almost as widely as before the Act in the building of new or substantially reconstructed premises.

Awareness of the failure of Sections 4 – 6 of the Act led Alf Morris, while Minister, to appoint a committee to investigate ways of improving access for disabled people. This committee, set up in 1977, the year of the Queen's Silver Jubilee and known as the Silver Jubilee Committee, reported in 1979.[7]

The Committee had neither the time nor the resources at its disposal to make a systematic study of man-made impediments to the free movement of disabled people in Britain, but relied on reports from organizations concerned with the welfare of disabled people and from a number of handicapped people individually. The overriding picture that emerged was one of thoughtless disregard for the needs of disabled people rather than callous determination to exclude them from public places. There were, however, some distressing examples of something very like the latter attitude, as in the case of one cinema manager who refused admission to a disabled woman ostensibly on the grounds of safety, but when pressed he declared that he simply did not want people in wheelchairs in the cinema. In another case a dance hall manager refused to allow in a young man in a wheelchair, saying that there was no point in letting him in as he could not dance.

The Silver Jubilee Committee found that the access provisions of the Chronically Sick and Disabled Persons Act were not known at all widely among property developers, and even where they were known, the waiver Clause permitted them to be ignored. There was no way of enforcing the requirement that the needs of disabled people be considered, and no way of deciding what it was both 'practicable and reasonable' to expect. Quite soon after the Act was passed one authority had refused to approve plans for a supermarket with a cinema above on the grounds that Section 4 had not been complied with, but this decision was overturned on appeal because the developers had argued, with very little supporting evidence, that on grounds of economy and safety it was neither practicable nor reasonable to provide access for disabled people to the proposed cinema. With no other basis on which to determine what was practicable and reasonable in the circumstances, the appeal was allowed, discouraging any further attempts to enforce the access provisions by withholding planning permission.

The most hopeful approach to improving access is probably by means of the building regulations imposed by the Department of Environment. If these were to be framed in such a way as to include a requirement to conform to the British Standard Code of Practice on access for disabled people to buildings (which was revised in 1979), there could be much tighter control of access facilities in new buildings. The Department of the Environment has the power to introduce this requirement into building regulations, and was known to be discussing the matter in 1979, but no decision had been announced at the time of going to press. However, even if the regulations did require observance of the British Standard Code of Practice, there would have to be a waiver Clause in order to allow for exceptional circumstances. None the less, it might be expected that the waiver Clause would be invoked exceptionally rather than routinely, as seems to be the case now. Moreover, if the British Standard Code of Practice on access for disabled people were to become more widely known as a result of a revision of building regulations, this in itself could be of considerable benefit to disabled people. According to the Silver Jubilee Committee, many of the man-made impediments to mobility were attributable to ignorance rather than wilful disregard of the needs of disabled people. Consequently, any increase in general awareness of the problems of access ought to reduce the number of barriers to mobility.

A point that recurred in a number of the submissions sent to the Silver Jubilee Committee related to the effect of recent fire and safety regulations on the accessibility of buildings to disabled people. It was reported that fire doors were frequently too heavy for disabled persons to open, and that admission to above-ground premises had often been refused to people in wheelchairs, even where there was a lift, because safety regulations forbade the use of lifts to leave a building when there was a fire. The Committee urged that further consideration should be given to the ways in which fire and safety regulations, designed to protect the public, adversely affected the quality of life of disabled people.

There could be no complacency, after the Silver Jubilee Committee's report, about the opportunities for disabled people to move about within their neighbourhoods despite the requirements of Sections 4 – 6 in the Chronically Sick and Disabled Persons Act. There was no doubt that the physical limitations of impaired people were only part, and often not the major part, of the handicap they suffered. Most of the barriers to mobility created by buildings designed without regard to the needs of disabled people, or by safety regulations that took account only of the able-bodied, were due to ignorance or thoughtlessness. Their effect, however was to discriminate against disabled people as far as the availability of facilities and opportunities was concerned.

One of the last actions undertaken by Alf Morris as Minister with special responsibility for disabled people was to establish in April 1979, just a month before the Government fell, a new committee to carry on where the Silver Jubilee Committee had left off. The committee was to be known as the Committee on Restrictions Against Disabled People (CORAD), and it was to look at the whole issue of discrimination against disabled people. The possibility of resulting legislation was not discounted. The chairman of CORAD, Mr Peter Large, MBE, said at the first meeting of CORAD held on April 5th 1979:

> In my opinion, one of the gravest threats to disabled people today arises not from malevolent, direct discrimination but from indirect and often inadvertent discrimination – discrimination by default, ignorance or apathy. The former is out in the open and thus easier to combat. The latter just happens. Nobody is really to blame because nobody has any responsibility to safeguard the rights of disabled people or any need to take account of these rights in deciding what to do or not do.
>
> For example, nobody intended fire and safety precautions to prevent disabled people from working or studying or enjoying themselves. But that is exactly what they are doing. Nobody intends

Codes of Practice covering fire precautions to prevent disabled people from working or shopping or living in certain places. But that is exactly what will happen if steps are not taken to call a halt to what I regard as an insane quest for unobtainable ultimate safety ....

Our job, as I see it, is to help correct those past practical mistakes and to devise means of avoiding similar mistakes in the future so that nobody has any excuse for discriminating against disabled people. Somehow we have to devise a means of preventing society riding rough shod over the rights of disabled people. Whether this requires the club or the carrot, education, exhortation or legislation, remains to be seen.

The limited success of existing anti-discrimination legislation, relating to sex and race, does not encourage much optimism about the possibility of legislation to prohibit discrimination on grounds of disability, particularly if, as Peter Large suggests, much of the discrimination is inadvertent, with no identifiable culprit. Much more necessary is a fundamental change of attitude, from that of regarding disabled individuals as marginal people set apart from the normal population, to one of understanding that the general public includes people across the whole range of bodily and mental fitness, with no clear dividing line between an able-bodied majority and a disabled minority. We are all one people.

Participation

One of the ways of ensuring that the interests of handicapped people are borne in mind is for disabled individuals to participate as fully as possible in a range of planning, advisory, and administrative activities.

Sections 9 – 15 of the Chronically Sick and Disabled Persons Act were designed to facilitate this type of participation by disabled people in spheres of planning and policy making that are of direct relevance to their welfare. For example, it was stipulated that the composition of each of the Central Advisory Committee on War Pensions, the Housing Advisory Committee, the National Insurance Advisory Committee and the Industrial Injuries Council should include at least one disabled person. Other bodies, such as the Youth Executive and the consultative committees of the gas and electricity services, public transport and the Post Office, were required to have one member with awareness of the special needs of disabled people. In these areas of activity the existence of the 'statutory' disabled member or spokesman has been accepted.

Section 15 of the Act, however, imposed a blanket requirement on local authorities setting up any committee whose membership was not restricted to local authority officials or councillors to appoint at least one disabled person as a member. There is no published information on the extent to which this general rubric has been observed by local authorities. In 1976 a question was asked in the Commons about the implementation of Section 15; the reply was to the effect that no information was available.[8] Subsequently, the Minister for the welfare of disabled people, Alf Morris, began to collect information on how local authorities had given effect to Section 15, but this material had not been collated and published by the time he left office in 1979. He pursued the matter in Opposition, but in response to his questions he was informed by his successor, Reg Prentice, that it would involve unreasonable expense to collect information about the numbers of disabled people serving on local authority committees, and that such information as had been collected 'was not in a form that would be meaningful if published'.[9]

The degree to which Section 15 has had any effect on the participation in community affairs of disabled people must, therefore, remain a mystery. Doubts about the extent to which disabled people are involved in local authority committee work reduce the confidence with which we might assume that their views are fully considered when local authorities plan priorities and implement economies that affect their welfare.

Even if there were no discrimination against them, it must be acknowledged that the majority of disabled people are unlikely to participate energetically in shaping the affairs of the community, simply because the majority are elderly, female and poor – all characteristics associated with a low community participation rate.[10] The burden of community activity is bound to fall on the relatively small number of younger, well-educated and alert disabled people. They are then open to the accusation that they are not typical of the majority of disabled people, whose interests they are able to represent no better than could any well-informed able-bodied person. Indeed, it could be argued that the experience of a disabled individual might lead him to concentrate on the problems with which he is familiar, to the exclusion of factors that might affect those with other disabilities in differing circumstances, whereas an able-bodied person would have no such bias. Furthermore, the very concern to have disabled spokesmen for disabled people emphasized by the Chronically Sick and Disabled Persons Act might appear to give the views of a disabled person on a committee particular weight, so that bias would be difficult to counter. The requirement might appear to suggest that one disabled person may be deemed able to speak for all other disabled people by some mysterious process of divination through affinity — why else should there be a statutory requirement for his presence?

These reservations about the wisdom of pursuing the objective of having disabled members on committees concerned with affairs that affect the lives of disabled people are based on two assumptions, neither of which is well-founded. The first is that such disabled committee members are there to represent all disabled people; and the second is that there is a plentiful supply of able-bodied people who are well-informed about the special needs and difficulties of disabled people.

The Silver Jubilee Committee showed how ill-informed the majority of the public was about the needs of disabled people, although when these were pointed out there was a general willingness to be helpful and considerate. It is for these reasons that a disabled member of a committee is likely to have an important part to play — not as a representative of disabled people, which he cannot be and was surely never intended to be, but as one who can remind his ill-informed but well-intentioned fellow committee members of some of the particular requirements of some disabled people. Any good committee will then be alerted to the need to inform itself further on the issues involved.

The normality of disablement

It has been argued elsewhere in this chapter that the disabled do not constitute a distinct group separate from the normal majority. Nearly every one of us suffers from some physical or mental under-development or imperfection due to age, disease or accident. For most of us during most of our lives these imperfections do not impede, to any noticeable extent, our use of the built environment. We may, for example, find a smaller house with fewer stairs more comfortable to live in as time goes by and imperfections increase. We may well come to find ourselves excluded from some community activities; with advancing years, shortness of breath, slack muscles or overweight exclude most of us from the sporting activities of the community, and for others colour blindness may have put many local art facilities out of range of enjoyment all their lives. These degrees of impairment come well within the 'normal' range, and it is difficult to pin-point exactly the stage at which normal imperfections become disablement. Yet for most of us, if we live long enough, more and more of our built environment will become inconvenient, even inaccessible, and participation in more and more community activities will become impossible for us. At some point we shall pass from being normal to being disabled.

Disability is, therefore, part of normal life for many of us, but it is generally a feature of ageing and most usually comes at a time of life when there is in any case a gradual withdrawal from involvement in a number of aspects of community life, such as family responsibilities, employment and, often, public affairs. It is easy then for the majority of us, not yet having made the transition from imperfection to disability, to forget the needs of those who have already withdrawn from so much of community activity when we make our plans for new shopping precincts, or self-service garages, or public lavatories with steps to the entrance. Through our forgetfulness we make the built environment even more inhospitable and exclude even more people from normal activities.

It is this process that we may hope to check by ensuring that disabled people do have a voice on committees and in inquiries and can remind us, before we have gone too far with our plans, that some of us are already disabled and that nearly all of us will be one day, if we live long enough.

NOTES

1. J. R. Buckle, *Work and Housing of Impaired Persons in Great Britain*, HMSO, London 1971.
2. *Housing and Construction Statistics No. 29*, First Quarter 1979, HMSO, London 1979.

3. Selwyn Goldsmith, *Mobility Housing*, Conference Proceedings of the 2nd European Conference of Rehabilitation International, NAIDEX, Sevenoaks, Kent, 1978.
4. *Housing and Construction Statistics.*
5. See A. Harris, C. R. W. Smith and E. Head, *Income and Entitlement to Supplementary Benefit of Impaired People in Great Britain*, HMSO, London, 1972.
6. Housing Development Directorate Occasional Paper 3/78, *Housing Services for Disabled People*, Department of Environment, 1978.
7. Silver Jubilee Committee Report on improving access for disabled people, *Can Disabled People Go Where You Go?*, DHSS, 1979.
8. *H. C. Deb.*, vol. 912, cols. *285 – 6.*
9. *H. D. Deb.*, vol. 980, cols. *358 – 9*; *H. C. Deb.*, vol. 980, cols. *286 – 7.*
10. J. Blondel, *Voters, Parties and Leaders*, Penguin, Harmondsworth, 1963, p. 56.

CHAPTER TEN

In Retrospect

High expectations

The Chronically Sick and Disabled Persons Act, 1970 received the Royal Assent only hours before the Government was dissolved. That it should have been squeezed through in this way, when other important Government measures such as the Crossman National Superannuation and Social Insurance Bill were lost shows how great was the support for, and interest in, Alf Morris's Bill. In view of Alf Morris's success in cultivating support for his Bill within Parliament, it is impossible to be sure that it would have been lost without clamorous public support for completing the measure, but it seems very likely that the work of pressure groups of and for disabled people in securing publicity for the Bill played a considerable part in convincing the outgoing Government that the measure should be among the few to be completed as a matter of urgency in the last few days of the administration.

When, eventually, the Bill completed its final stages, there were quite extraordinary congratulatory speeches in both Houses, as we have seen, and there is no doubt that there were widespread expectations of a marked improvement in the quality of life of disabled people as a result of the Chronically Sick and Disabled Persons Act. Yet, looking back, it is hard to understand the tremendous euphoria. There were, of course, some notes of caution. The *Financial Times*, for example, while welcoming the measure as 'a significant step forward in provision for the care of the disabled people who live among us', went on to explain that, as a private Member's measure, the Act could not provide for any major increase in expenditure on the welfare of disabled people. Its main effect would be 'an administrative tidying up that should lead to better services from local authorities'.[1] This very reasonable assessment of what might be expected from the Act was, however, entirely swamped by the mass of enthusiastic predictions of a new era dawning for the disabled person. Unrealistically high expectations were expressed even by people who well knew the financial limitations on private Member's Bills. One can only conclude that these high hopes were based on an unquestioning faith in continued economic growth, which would permit local authorities to allocate ever-increasing amounts of money in real terms to the provision of services for disabled people. In the climate of the 1980s such faith in economic growth is barely credible, but it was commonplace in 1970.

An alternative explanation for these high hopes was suggested by Barbara Castle in a speech she made to a conference of the British Association of Social Workers in 1972.[2] Referring to the frustrated expectations of disabled people, she asserted that the Chronically Sick and Disabled Persons Act definitely implied expenditure. As a private Member's measure, it could never have reached the Statute Book, she claimed, if the Government of the day had not passed a Money Resolution that, as Barbara Castle put it, expressed 'the will of the Government to find resources for it'. Unfortunately, she explained, the Labour Government fell before the form and extent of those promised resources had been spelled out, and the incoming Conservative Government had simply not made available the necessary resources that the previous Government had intended should be committed to meeting the demands stimulated by the Act.

It is doubtful if this can be the correct explanation, as even when the Conservative Government was replaced by a Labour administration in 1974 and Alf Morris, sponsor of the Chronically Sick and Disabled Persons Act became Minister for the Disabled, there was still no clear commitment to the provision of financial resources by the Government to the local authorities for the purpose of providing the services and facilities specified in the Act. The Money Resolution remains a commitment in principle, so ambiguously worded as to avoid any definite promise of the sums that would have to be expended if local authorities were to meet in full all their new obligations under the terms of the Act. The wording of the Resolution is set out below.

MONEY ORDER RESOLUTION   February 3rd 1970
That, for the purpose of any Act of the present session to make
further provision with respect to the welfare of chronically sick and
disabled persons, it is expedient to authorize the payment out of
moneys provided by Parliament of any increase in the sums payable
out of moneys so provided under any other enactment which is
attributable to any provisions of that Act imposing a duty on a local
authority having functions under Section 29 of the National
Assistance Act 1948 to make arrangements in the exercise of their
functions under that section if they are satisfied in the case of any
person ordinarily resident in the authority's area who is a person to
whom that section applies that it is necessary to make those
arrangements in order to meet the needs of that person.[3]

The meaning of the Resolution appears to be that if a local
authority incurred additional expenses as a result of the fact that
the Chronically Sick and Disabled Persons Act made mandatory
the provision of services for disabled people that were only
permissive functions under Section 29 of the National Assistance
Act, the Government could make an increased allocation of money
to that local authority, presumably by increasing the rate support
grant. The Resolution does not say that the Government would
make additional money available; nor if this were to happen, does
it specify the basis upon which the addition would be calculated.
It is clear that in making the Money Order Resolution the
Government of the day was signifying its willingness to see the
Chronically Sick and Disabled Persons Bill become law, since the
Bill had no chance of enactment without the Order. It is less clear
from the wording of the Resolution that, as Mrs Castle claimed in
1972, the Government intended at that time to make sufficient
financial allocation to local authorities to enable them to meet all
the expectations aroused by the passing of the Act. What is now
certain is that under first a Conservative and then a Labour
administration the Money Order Resolution did not lead to an
increased financial allocation to local authorities that was
specifically ear-marked and sufficient to promote services to
disabled people to the degree which would satisfy all demand.

The reality

Chapter Eight, on the development of services covered by Section 2
of the Chronically Sick and Disabled Persons Act, examines the
improvements in provision and the existing shortfalls. The

possibility is that the gap between need and provision is currently widening. The economic cuts in spending imposed on local authorities at the end of the 1970s were presented by the Government spokesmen as designed to trim extravagances and restrict expansion. Reg Prentice, who had replaced Alf Morris as Minister for the Disabled with the change of Government in 1979, described the cuts that local authorities were required to make as reducing the 'spending plans that they have in the pipeline', but he added that the DHSS was also requesting local authorities to avoid making cuts in their services to the chronically sick, the disabled and the elderly. Reg Prentice declared, 'I hope and believe that this can happen throughout the country'.[4]

His hopes, however, were ill-founded. Local authority social services departments, together with education services, had to bear their share of the cuts in expenditure, and the chronically sick and disabled and the elderly form the bulk of recipients of their services. The planned increases in expenditure were those that would be required to meet price rises and salary increases already announced and to satisfy the needs of the increased numbers of elderly people in the population, among whom are many with disabling conditions. A further source of increased demand on local authority social services is the policy of the National Health Service to transfer to community care a number of mentally handicapped persons for whom hospital care is unnecessary and inappropriate.

Without the planned increases in expenditure on social services designed to meet the increased demand resulting from greater numbers of handicapped persons in the community, it was absolutely certain that there would be reductions in the amount of assistance that could be made available to such persons. By the 1980s, therefore, any improvements in the provision of personal social services for chronically sick and disabled persons achieved under Section 2 of the Act were being eroded.

Chapter Nine has looked at the development of housing and accommodation for disabled people, and although some progress can be seen to have taken place in the years following the passing of the Chronically Sick and Disabled Persons Act, it was slow. Special provision for disabled people in the public housing sector, as encouraged by Section 4 of the Act, did not materialize to any extent until the mid-1970s, and after a few years, during which a useful number of special dwellings and mobility housing units were constructed, cuts in local authority expenditure effected a virtual halt in the expansion of council dwellings suitable for occupation by disabled people. In the sphere of housing, as in the area of personal social services, the effects of the Chronically Sick and Disabled Persons Act have been modest, and the indications are that the 1980s may see a reversal of even the slight trend towards the increased availability of suitable dwellings for rent by disabled people.

Residential accommodation, which is still, for most handicapped people, the only alternative to living in the community with minimal support, was not the subject of any specific provision in the Act. Sections 17 and 18 of the Act, however, required health authorities and local authorities to make returns of the numbers of handicapped persons under the age of 65 who were accommodated in units normally used wholly or mainly for the care of persons over that age. These Clauses were inserted because of the concern of the sponsors of the Act about the numbers of younger handicapped people who were condemned to years of existence in the company of very old, frail and often senile people in geriatric units because there were no special facilities in which they could more appropriately be accommodated.

In the years following the passing of the Chronically Sick and Disabled Persons Act young chronic sick units were established within the National Health Service, and local authorities opened homes and hostels for younger disabled people. In the second half of the 1970s both these forms of expansion slowed and finally stopped. Health authorities began to doubt the usefulness of young chronic sick units, since patients in need of hospital treatment were most suitably accommodated within existing hospital provision, and those with residual handicaps for which there was no treatment were not appropriately housed in hospital units of any sort. There was, perhaps, a need for specialized rehabilitation units in the National Health Service, and some young Chronic sick units tried to move in this direction, leaving the residential care of disabled people to local authorities. In the local authority sphere the provision of accommodation on the basis of a distinction between those under and those over the age of 65 was perceived as largely irrelevant to the issue of matching facilities to the needs and aspirations of disabled people.

Even before economic recession called a halt to the expansion of local authority services there had been a pause in the process of establishing more residential accommodation specifically for younger disabled people in order to take stock of the emerging situation. With severe financial restaints imposed on local authority expenditure at the end of the decade, the pause in the development of residential care accommodation became a cessation. Yet there was no corresponding arrest of demand. The longevity of those already admitted to residential care, coupled with the lack of expansion of provision, meant that by the end of the 1970s too few vacancies were available to meet the demand from those who had become severely disabled. Some of this demand for residential care might have been averted through the provision of more supporting services in the community, but the cuts in local authority budgets ensured that the halt in developing residential facilities for disabled people was not offset by the expansion of alternative provision to assist those remaining at home.

What difference has the Act made?

The concrete improvements that have been achieved as a direct result of the Chronically Sick and Disabled Persons Act are real but have added up to only a modest advance in the quality of life for disabled people. They have certainly not amounted to a new era for handicapped people and their families, or a passport to a vastly more understanding and welcoming society, as many optimistically claimed at the moment of triumph when the Act received the Royal Assent.

It would be wrong to judge the Act solely by the effects directly attributable to its various sections, however. There have been a number of development in the sphere of welfare for disabled persons since the Act. In 1977 Alf Morris, while Minister for the Disabled, produced in response to a question in the House a long list of measures or regulations introduced since the Act that were designed to assist disabled people. The public concern that was aroused at the time that the Act was being widely debated and discussed created a climate of opinion in which further measures of assistance, in areas not directly covered by the Act, were able to gain support and to become established. Perhaps the cultivation of this favourable attitude has been the most important consequence of the Chronically Sick and Disabled Persons Act. It represented an unequivocal statement of collective concern for the welfare of disabled people, expressed by our representative legislature, on behalf of all of us. The personal tragedy of disablement was acknowledged to have implications not only for the individual and his immediate family, but also for society as a whole. Disablement of a fellow citizen was recognized to impose a duty on society to ameliorate, as far as possible, those handicapping restrictions on activities and the enjoyment of life that disabled people experienced as a result not of their functional loss but of social factors such as poverty or unsuitable buildings, which we had the knowledge and ability to alter. Society may, in fact, have expended too little in the way of resources and effort to adjust the environment, as much as many would wish, to meet the needs of disabled people, but the acceptance of an obligation to move in this direction has never been challenged since the passing of the Act.

The acknowledgment of a duty is significant, even when that duty is not fully discharged, because it confers reciprocal rights. Indeed, it is arguable that the very ambiguities of the Chronically Sick and Disabled Persons Act in respect of entitlement to specific services and facilities have emphasized the Act as accepting in principle the rights of disabled people as citizens to full participation in the community. Certainly, in the years since the passing of the Act we have heard more and more about the rights of disabled people in terms that have made it plain that the rights referred to are not derived from any specific provisions of the Act. The Chairman of CORAD, for example, called the existing fire and safety regulations in Britain 'an insane quest for unobtainable ultimate safety' that was interfering with the rights of disabled people to work or shop or live in certain places, or to enjoy certain plays, concerts or films.[5] This criticism of a piece of legislation designed to protect the majority on the grounds that it infringed the more fundamental rights of a minority was reported quite widely in the national press. It provoked no angry response, which suggests that there is now a widespread acceptance of the principle that the rights of disabled people must be taken into account in framing any regulations and, further that in some situations measures that might be desirable in the interests of the majority could constitute such an encroachment on the basic rights of disabled citizens as to make them unacceptable.

One of these basic rights about which we have heard much more in recent years is the disabled person's right to love.[6]. This right was originally proclaimed to an incredulous and rather shocked public, which had formerly behaved as though any severely disabling condition, no matter what its nature, automatically desexed its victim. Once the disabled person's right to love was accepted by society, it became the justification for arguing that social arrangements and social provisions should be ordered in such a way as to facilitate, or at least not to obstruct, the realization of this right. Residential accommodation, for example, needs to be designed in such a way as to permit the establishment of close personal relationships, including marriage. This means, in effect, single rooms (more expensive to provide than wards or dormitories), in which the occupant can enjoy privacy with his or her chosen intimates, and the availability of residential accommodation for couples, perhaps for families.

Organizations of and for disabled people have been in the forefront of the campaign to secure disabled people's rights. This campaign has been able to take for granted that a disabled person *has* rights in order to concentrate on documenting the disadvantages endured by disabled people that preclude the realization of these rights — disadvantages that are potentially avoidable by collective action. The implicit (and often explicit) implication is that society has a duty to provide resources to reduce or eliminate such disadvantages.

This confident assertion of disabled person's rights is a recent phenomenon. Even the disabled servicemen of both world wars, assured of the gratitude of the whole population, were far less vociferous in making claim to anything more than pensions and compassionate physical care of the very dependent. It does suggest that the Chronically Sick and Disabled Persons Act, which amounted to an official acceptance of the fact that society has a duty towards its disabled citizens, has helped to change the attitudes both of able-bodied people towards their disabled fellows and of disabled people towards themselves and their legitimate aspirations.

Attitudes and the law

It is difficult to establish whether or not law can change attitudes. It was, for example, widely denied at the time of the Race Relations Acts that attitudes could be altered by legislation, and similar criticisms have been made of attempts to ensure equal opportunities for women by means of legislation. On the other hand, the view has commonly been expressed that changes in the law making divorce more easily available have generated irresponsible attitudes towards marriage and family life.

In fact, of course, laws seek to regulate behaviour, not attitudes, although clearly the two are related. Much of our behaviour reflects our attitudes, but laws can constrain individuals to act in ways contrary to the inclinations that they derive from their attitudes and beliefs. In the case of a law-abiding citizen, when such a situation arises he must either endure a permanent sense of constraint or rethink his attitudes to the point at which they incline him to act in the way that the law requires. It is surely in this sense that some people's attitudes may be changed by the law. Some, for example, who held the attitude that severely disabled people should be kept out of the mainstream of society, which was not geared to accommodate them, were constrained by the Chronically Sick and Disabled Persons Act to behave as if they believed disabled persons *should* be in the mainstream of a society that had an obligation to facilitate their participation. After a period of time of acting in this way the likelihood is that attitudes will be gradually modified to fit in with the new pattern of behaviour.

It may be argued, however, that the Chronically Sick and Disabled Persons Act could not alone have effected a change in the attitudes of the majority of the population, since without sympathetic support the Bill would have failed to become law. Indeed, it is arguable that in a democratic country like Britain no measure can be enacted without the support of, or at least the absence of opposition from, the majority of the population. Therefore, any legislation must be a reflection of widely held existing attitudes rather than an instrument for modifying attitudes. Even if it is agreed that a strong Government can use its parliamentary majority to push through one or two measures that do not have wide support in the country as a whole, any private Member's Bill would certainly have to attract a large measure of general support, and to encounter little outright opposition, if it were to survive the strict time constraints on such Bills and have any chance at all of reaching the Statute Book.

The Chronically Sick and Disabled Persons Bill clearly attracted tremendous support during its passage through Parliament. The occasion it afforded for the dissemination of information and publicity about disabled people, which was exploited most skilfully, increased public awareness and sympathy already widespread in a society sensible of its debt to the war disabled and conscious that, with rising numbers of road traffic accidents and greater longevity, every citizen runs a considerable risk of becoming disabled at some time in his life. It may reasonably be assumed that the Act, aimed at increasing the help available to disabled people, reflected prevailing sympathies in 1970. Must it therefore be concluded that the only attitudes that it could have influenced were those of a minority of unsympathetic people, leaving untouched the views of the vast majority? Surely not. The greater visibility of disabled individuals going about their ordinary business, and the more frequent contact of able-bodied people with them as work colleagues, fellow shoppers, committee men, or neighbours that has been encouraged by the Act, must have contributed to a revised perception of disabled people. There has been a growing readiness to redefine the possible limits of participation in society by disabled people. This in turn has indicated the need for further improvements in facilities and services in order to promote this fuller participation.

The interaction between general attitudes and action since the introduction of the Chronically Sick and Disabled Persons Act, in other words, has been a two-way process leading both to new provisions not covered by the Act and to new attitudes not widely held at the time the Act was passed. This beneficient spiral, however, can progress only within the framework of society's overall values and objectives.

It has been argued elsewhere[7] that the overriding value of modern industrial society is that of economic rationality, which subjects every belief or proposal to the test of whether or not it would be conducive to net economic prosperity. In the case of services and facilities that are needed in order to ensure that the functional losses of disabled people are not compounded with environmental disadvantages, society has been willing to commit resources provided the primary objective of economic progress is not threatened. When, as in the late 1970s and in the 1980s the country's economic growth is in jeopardy, the needs of disabled people are frankly subordinated to those of the economy. The Secretary of State for Social Services, speaking at a conference held in 1980 to consider the problems of elderly people, emphasized that restoring the country's economic vigour must be the top priority; help for the elderly and the disabled, he claimed, should be curtailed or even reduced until it can be provided without limiting the economic growth of the country as a whole.[8] His view of social priorities was not challenged, even by elderly or disabled people and their supporters. The opposition to cuts in expenditure on services and facilities for disabled people was generally on the lines that the cuts would not, in the long run, save expenditure because they would make disabled people more isolated, more dependent, less productive and more expensive to support.

The propriety of this response by disabled people and their supporters to enforced economies is not being questioned here. What is asserted is that the Chronically Sick and Disabled Persons Act has proved powerless to avert reductions in provision for disabled people. Its influence on attitudes seems to have been limited to creating a greater willingness to examine evidence that attempts to show that meeting the needs of disabled people, though costing money initially, may save it eventually, resulting in a net gain to society. There also seems to be a greater willingness to give disabled people the benefit of any doubt about the accuracy of the complicated cost – benefit calculations that are made.

These may seem unremarkable achievements for a measure that was hailed as a charter for disabled people marking the dawn of a new era, but that in retrospect is seen to have led only to modest improvements in services and to some increase in sympathy among the general public with the aspirations of disabled people. But has any piece of social legislation achieved more?

To say that the Chronically Sick and Disabled Persons Act 1970 has not revolutionized the values of society but has left us counting the cost of care much as before, except that there are some new items in the sum, is to underplay the very real contribution the Act has made to improving opportunities for disabled people. This contribution should not be measured solely in terms of the increase in services directly specified in the Act, though the benefit here has been real enough to those disabled men and women who have been provided with aids, adaptations or telephones, assisted to go on holiday or supported by help in the home. One must also take account of the further measures to promote the welfare of disabled people that have been succesfully introduced in the climate of greater understanding that is attributable, at least in part, to the Chronically Sick and Disabled Persons Act.

NOTES

1. *Financial Times*, March 19th 1970.
2. Address by the Rt Hon Barbara Castle, PC, MP, delivered at the Conference of the British Association of Social Workers, October, 1972.
3. *H. C. Deb.*, vol. 795, col. 381.
4. Mr Reginald Prentice, MP, speaking at the Annual Conference of the Leonard Cheshire Foundation, September, 1979.
5. Mr Peter Large, MBE, Chairman, CORAD, reported in *Cheshire Smile*, Spring 1979.
6. See, for example, Wendy Greengross, *Entitled to Love*, National Marriage Guidance Council, London, 1976.
7. E. Topliss, *Provision for the Disabled*, 2nd edn., Basil Blackwell and Martin Robertson, Oxford and London, 1979.
8. *The Times*, February 8th 1980.

Appendix

Chronically Sick and Disabled Persons Bill
Chronically Sick and Disabled Persons Act 1970

Chronically Sick and Disabled Persons Bill

ARRANGEMENT OF CLAUSES

[Bill 21]   A   44/4

ii   *Chronically Sick and Disabled Persons*

A

B I L L

T O

Make further provisions with respect to the welfare A.D. 1969
of chronically sick and disabled persons; and for
connected purposes.

BE IT ENACTED by the Queen's most Excellent Majesty, by and
with the advice and consent of the Lords Spiritual and
Temporal, and Commons, in this present Parliament
assembled, and by the authority of the same, as follows:—

Appendix A

5   *Assistance by local authorities to chronically*
sick and disabled

1.—(1) Subject to the provisions of this section, it shall be the Registration
duty of every local health authority to maintain a register of all of chronically
chronically sick and disabled persons resident in their area, sick and
10 other than those persons who have been admitted to a hospital persons.
for long term treatment.

(2) Subject to the provisions of this section, it shall be the duty
of every hospital to maintain a register of all chronically sick and
disabled persons admitted to that hospital for long term treatment.

15   (3) The Secretary of State shall make regulations providing
for the manner in which registers shall be kept, the maintenance
of confidentiality, the particulars which shall be recorded in
them, and for the removal of names or transfer of names from
one register to another.

Appendix B

20   **2.** It shall be the duty of every local health authority and Information
every hospital to provide, not less than once in every six months, to be given
to every chronically sick or disabled person who is registered in to chronically
their register, or in the case of such a person under the age of 18, disabled
to his parent or guardian, information in whatever form is persons.
25 appropriate to the individual regarding—

　　　(i) any aids and appliances;
　　　(ii) any domestic help;
　　　(iii) any financial benefits;

[Bill 21]   A 2   44/4

P TO

(iv) any facilities provided under section 3 of this Act;

(v) any other form of assistance, whether physical, pecuniary or otherwise;

which they are or may be entitled to use or receive by reason of their sickness or disablement.

Special provision for disabled by local health authorities.

3.—(1) It shall be the duty of every local health authority to—

(i) provide practical assistance for disabled persons in their homes;

(ii) provide, or assist in obtaining wireless, library and similar recreational facilities for disabled persons; 10

(iii) provide for disabled persons lectures, games, outings and other recreational facilities in social centres or elsewhere;

(iv) provide facilities for, and assistance to, disabled persons in travelling to and from their homes to participate in any of the services provided under the council or for 15 any other similar purpose approved by the council in this respect;

(v) assist disabled persons in arranging for the carrying out of any works of adaptation in their homes or the provision of any additional facilities, designed to secure 20 the greater comfort or convenience of such persons, and if the council so determine defray wholly or partly any expenses incurred in the carrying out of any such works or in the provision of any such facilities;

(vi) facilitate the taking of holidays by disabled persons, in 25 particular at holiday homes, whether provided by the council or otherwise, or provided or established by any other body, and if the council so determine defray any expenses incurred in or in connection with the taking of such holidays; 30

(vii) provide training facilities for persons who can increase their hearing perception by means of a hearing aid.

(2) It shall be the duty of every local health authority to provide such sheltered workshops as the Secretary of State may approve in which disabled persons may be employed 35 in suitable work or may be trained in pursuance of the Disabled Persons Employment Acts 1944 and 1958 and to provide suitable means of transport to and from the workshops where this is necessary.

(3) It shall be the duty of every local health authority, in 40 consultation with the Secretary of State, to assist under supervision disabled persons who are capable of earning at least such reasonable weekly sum as the council may determine, by the production of saleable goods or the tendering of useful services, to engage in activities to that end in their own homes, or elsewhere 45 other than in sheltered workshops.

(4) Every local health authority shall have power to make such arrangements as the authority may from time to time determine for providing meals and recreation for disabled persons in their homes or elsewhere and may employ as their agent for
5 the purpose of this subsection any voluntary organisation whose activities consist in or include the provision of meals or recreation for disabled persons.

(5) The Secretary of State may make regulations providing for scales of expenditure by local authorities on the provision of
10 equipment and appliances to chronically sick and disabled persons.

4.—(1) Every local housing authority shall, within such period Housing and at such times as he may determine, submit to the Minister needs of the of Housing and Local Government proposals for securing that disabled. adequate and sufficient provision is made, including the adapta-
15 tion of existing properties, for the housing requirements of those in their areas who are chronically sick or disabled persons.

(2) The Minister may require local housing authorities to carry out the said proposals with or without modifications as approved by him.

20 (3) Local housing authorities may, in carrying out their duties under this section of this Act, make arrangements with hospital authorities established under the National Health Service Acts for the provision of housing accommodation on land owned or leased by any such hospital authority.

25 (4) The Secretary of State may require any Regional Hospital Board to make reports from time of hospital land surplus to that Board's requirements and which may be used for housing development to benefit the chronically sick and disabled.

5. It shall be the duty of every local health authority to report Provision
30 to the Secretary of State within six months of the passing of this of toilet Act and thereafter at intervals of two years, on the provisions facilities. they have made to ensure that sufficient toilet facilities exist in or within easy access of the principal shopping centres in their area, for use by disabled persons who are confined to wheelchairs or
35 who are semi-ambulant, and that the whereabouts of such toilet facilities are adequately signposted and publicised.

6.—(1) It shall be the duty of every local health authority to Access to provide, so far as is reasonably practicable, for disabled persons public who are confined to vehicles, means of access to and means of buildings.
40 circulation within, town halls, county halls, public libraries, public baths, and other public buildings in their area to which disabled persons may wish habitually to resort.

(2) Such means of access and circulation shall include:—

(i) reserved parking space for disabled drivers or severely disabled passengers both adjacent to and with an accessible approach to the building;

(ii) at least one accessible entrance to the building unimpeded   5
by steps;

(iii) internal circulation both horizonal and vertical, unimpeded by steps, including in a multi-storey building the provision of lifts large enough to take wheelchairs, and the avoidance of split levels, so that all parts of the 10
building used by the general public can be reached; and

(iv) accessible sanitary and cloakroom accommodation on at least one floor of the building.

Provision of information to local health authority.
7. It shall be the duty of every local education authority to furnish from time to time to the Social Work Department in 15
every local health authority information concerning any children who have attained the age of 14 years who have acquired disabilities, or whose disability was not apparent at birth.

Assessment of means.
8. Any officer of a local authority responsible for assessing for any purpose the means of a person or family of a person 20
suffering from disability shall take reasonable account of the additional expenses which may be incurred by that person or family by reason of that disability.

Travel concessions.
9. Persons suffering from severe visual defect short of blindness whose age does not exceed eighteen years shall be included in 25
the class of qualified persons to whom travel concessions may be granted under the Travel Concessions Acts 1955 and 1964,

1955 c. 26.
and accordingly in subsection (2) of section 1 of the Public Service Vehicles (Travel Concessions) Act 1955, after paragraph (*d*) there shall be inserted—   30

" (*dd*) persons suffering from severe visual defect short of blindness whose age does not exceed 18 years; "

Advisory committees, etc.

War pensions committees.
10. The Secretary of State shall cause to be convened an annual conference of war pensions committee chairmen in order to 35
report on the work of war pension committees for the war-disabled and their widows and to advise the Secretary of State on the execution of his duties in this regard.

Attendance allowance.
11. The Secretary of State shall establish an advisory council of not more than twelve persons to supervise the administration 40
of an attendance allowance for the severely disabled and to advise on its extension to other categories of disabled persons.

12. On any advisory committee established or to be established Housing to advise the Secretary of State on the provision and design of advisory houses there shall be included at least one member with experience committees. of work among and of the needs of the chronically sick and 5 disabled.

13. The National Insurance Advisory Committee shall include National at least one person with experience of work among and of the Insurance needs of the chronically sick and disabled. Advisory Committee.

14. The Industrial Injuries Advisory Council shall include at Industrial 10 least one person with experience of work among and of the Injuries needs of the chronically sick and disabled. Advisory Council.

15.—(1) Without prejudice to any other arrangements that Youth may be made by the Secretary of State, the Central Youth employment Employment Executive shall include at least one person with service. 15 special responsibility for the employment of young disabled persons.

(2) In the First Schedule to the Employment and Training Act 1948 c. 46. 1948 (National Youth Employment Council and Advisory Committees for Scotland and Wales) paragraph 1 shall be 20 amended by deleting " thirty-six " and inserting " thirty-seven ", and by adding at the end—

" (g) one person shall be appointed with experience of work among and the special needs of young disabled persons ".

National Health Service provisions

25 **16.**—(1) It shall be the duty of every local authority, from a Chiropody date to be determined by the Secretary of State, to make service. provision in their area for a chiropody service, including provision for treatment at health centres, in the premises of chiropodists, or where persons require it, in their own homes.

30 (2) A local health authority may, with the approval of the Secretary of State and from a date to be determined by him, recover from persons availing themselves of the service provided under this section such charges (if any) as the authority consider reasonable, having regard to the means of those persons.

35 (3) This section shall be construed as one with the provisions of Part III of the National Health Service Act 1946.   1946 c. 81.

17. Section 33 of the Health Services and Public Health Act Provision 1968 shall be amended— of vehicles for persons (*a*) in subsection (1) by adding at the end thereof the words— suffering 40   " Provided that any person appearing to the from physical medical practitioner with whom that person is defect or registered to be suffering from haemophilia shall be disability. 1968 c. 33.

6   *Chronically Sick and Disabled Persons*

eligible to be provided with a vehicle other than an
invalid carriage ";
(*b*) by inserting after subsection (1) the following section—
"(1A) Persons disabled for any reason other than
as a result of service in the armed forces during the   5
1914 World War and after 2nd September 1939 shall
have the like entitlement to vehicles other than invalid
carriages as persons entitled to vehicles as a result of
the said service"; and
(*c*) in subsection (7) by adding at the end thereof the words—   10
" and as from the passing of the Chronically Sick
and Disabled Persons Act 1969 shall mean a vehicle
as aforesaid including not less than two seats ".

Disabled
passengers.

18. The Secretary of State shall have power to provide a
vehicle to a person who is so severely disabled that he is unable   15
to drive it himself but who can designate a person to drive it on
his behalf.

Courses in
technical
equipment
of disabled.

19.—(1) It shall be the duty of every Regional Hospital Board
to provide, as respects their area, for medical practitioners
courses in the assessment of the need of disabled persons for   20
appliances and other technical equipment.

(2) The Secretary of State may make regulations for the
reimbursement on such terms as he may prescribe of Regional
Hospital Boards for any expenses they may incur in the provision
of the above-mentioned courses.   25

Admission
to geriatric
accommoda-
tion.

20.—(1) It shall be unlawful for any local health authority, or
any other local authority, or any hospital, or any other institution
providing accommodation for the elderly, to admit any younger
chronically sick person to, or keep any such person in, geriatric
accommodation, without the authority of the Secretary of State   30
granted within a period of three months from the date of
admission, or in the case of any such persons admitted to such
accommodation prior to the date on which this Act comes into
force, within three months from that date, and reports shall be
made to the Secretary of State every three months in such form   35
as he may prescribe of the numbers of such persons admitted
and kept in such accommodation and the reasons for their
admission and maintenance in such accommodation, and the
Secretary of State shall lay copies of the reports before Parliament.

(2) In this section "geriatric accommodation" means any   40
building, or any ward, room or section of any building, which
is wholly or mainly used for the accommodation of geriatric
patients.

(3) In this section " younger chronic sick " means any patient under 45 years who is receiving long-term care for a chronic disability or illness; and " long-term " covers patients likely to remain in hospital indefinitely or until death, and patients with
5 chronic disabilities or illnesses normally looked after at home but temporarily accommodated in hospital to help the family (with the exception of patients admitted to hospital for an episode of acute illness).

21. With regard to the training of persons to work with disabled Training
10 persons and in particular concerned with placement, sheltered of persons
employment, work at home or the training of the disabled, there working with
shall be established a Training Council with the following disabled
functions:— persons.

    (*a*) to supervise and review the content and extent of existing
15   training courses; and

    (*b*) to establish and conduct courses of training where no
        recognised courses at present exist.

Hearing

22. As from the passing of this Act it shall not be lawful for Employers not
20 any person offering employment to refuse employment to any to restrict
person on the sole ground that that person is partially deaf: offers of
employment.

Provided that in any action brought under this section it shall be a defence for an employer to show that a partially deaf person would be seriously impeded by reason of his disability
25 in the performance of the duties he was required to undertake.

23. It shall be the duty of the Secretary of State to provide for Training, etc.,
the training, education after the school-leaving age, and employ- of totally deaf.
ment of totally deaf persons.

24.—(1) There shall be established at a date to be determined Institute of
30 by the Secretary of State a body called the Institute of Hearing Hearing
Research (hereinafter called " the Institute ") which shall be a Research.
body corporate with perpetual succession and a common seal, and shall have the general function of co-ordinating and promoting research on hearing and assistance to the deaf and hard of hearing.

35   (2) The Secretary of State may make regulations after con-
sultation with such persons as he may choose relating to the conduct of the Institute's affairs, and the appointment, terms of service and remuneration of its officers.

8   *Chronically Sick and Disabled Persons*

Miscellaneous provisions

Use of
invalid
carriages on
highways.

25.—(1) In the case of a vehicle which is an invalid carriage complying with the prescribed requirements and which is being used in accordance with the prescribed conditions—

    (*a*) no statutory provision prohibiting or restricting the use 5
         of footways shall prohibit or restrict the use of that
         vehicle on a footway;

    (*b*) if the vehicle is mechanically propelled, it shall be treated

1960 c. 16.
1962 c. 59.
1967 c. 76.
1967 c. 30.

         for the purposes of the Road Traffic Act 1960, the Road
         Traffic Act 1962, the Road Traffic Regulation Act 1967 10
         and Part I of the Road Safety Act 1967 as not being a
         motor vehicle; and

1957 c. 51.

    (*c*) whether or not the vehicle is mechanically propelled, it
         shall be exempted from the requirements of the Road
         Transport Lighting Act 1957.   15

(2) In this section—

    " footway " means a way which is a footway, footpath or

1959 c. 25.

        bridleway within the meaning of the Highways Act 1959;

    " invalid carriage " means a vehicle, whether mechanically
        propelled or not, constructed or adapted for use for the 20
        carriage of one person, being a person suffering from
        some physical defect or disability;

    " prescribed " means prescribed by regulations made by the
        Minister of Transport;

    " statutory provision " means a provision contained in, or 25
        having effect under, any enactment.

(3) Any regulations made under this section shall be made by statutory instrument, may make different provision for different circumstances and shall be subject to annulment in pursuance of a Resolution of either House of Parliament.   30

Research and
development
undertaken by
Ministry of
Technology.

26.—(1) The Minister of Technology shall lay before Parliament an annual report showing what research and development programmes have been undertaken by, or on behalf of, the Ministry of Technology during the preceding year which are directly or indirectly for the benefit of disabled persons.   35

(2) Without prejudice to the generality of the foregoing subsection, the report may include a statement of work being done on the design, production and availability of appliances and technical equipment for the disabled.

Service
disability
pension.

27.—(1) Notwithstanding anything in any enactment or any 40 provision in any instrument having statutory effect heretofore made, an applicant for a disability pension arising out of service with any of the armed forces of the Crown, shall not, because of

delay in presenting the claim, be liable to satisfy any greater onus
of proof than that which relates to claims made without delay
unless the Medical Tribunal or Medical Appeals Tribunal shall
certify that it is established that the delay was unreasonable and
5 has resulted in grave and unnecessary difficulty to the respondent
to the claim in the preparation or presentation of the respondent's
answer to the claim.

(2) A medical tribunal or medical appeals tribunal shall not,
in hearing an application for a service disability pension on
10 the ground of continuing or recent recurrent incapacity, be
debarred by any previous decision of a tribunal as to the cause
of the disability or its extent from re-examining the whole of
such question or questions in the light of the evidence then
available or from making such determination of the case as
15 would, except solely for such previous determination, to them
have seemed just.

28. Where any chronically sick or disabled person requires Charges for
any special telephone equipment to enable him to make use of a telephone
telephone at his home, he shall not be required to pay more for equipment.
20 the installation or rental of such equipment, than is charged for
the installation and rental of a normal telephone.

29. The Minister of Posts and Telecommunications may Fees and
dispense with the whole or part of any sum which may be payable charges for
on the issue or renewal of any wireless or television licence if wireless
25 he is satisfied that the applicant is a chronically sick or disabled telegraphy
person confined to and resident in his own home; and accordingly licences.
subsection (2) of section 2 of the Wireless Telegraphy Act 1949, 1949 c. 54.
as amended by section 1 of the Wireless Telegraphy (Blind 1955 c. 7
Persons) Act 1955, shall be amended by inserting after the words (4 & 5 Eliz. 2).
30 " or in a school ", the words " or is a chronically sick or disabled
person confined to and resident in his own home ".

30. The earnings rule for the wife of any man drawing sickness Earnings
benefit for more than twenty-eight weeks shall be applied at rule for wife
the same rate as is applied in the case of retirement pension; of sick man.
35 and accordingly paragraph (*b*) of subsection (1) of section 43
of the National Insurance Act 1965 shall be amended by leaving 1965 c. 51.
out the words " that amount " and inserting in place thereof
the words " the amount above which earnings affect the rate of
retirement pension ".

40 **31.**—(1) It shall be the duty of every local education authority Provision
within three months of the passing of this Act and at such future of special
times as the Secretary of State may determine, to provide the educational
Secretary of State with information on the provision made by for the
that local education authority of special educational facilities for deaf–blind.
45 children who suffer the dual handicap of blindness and deafness.

10   *Chronically Sick and Disabled Persons*

(2) The arrangements made by a local education authority for the special eduational treatment of the deaf-blind shall, so far as is practicable, provide for the giving of such education in any school maintained or assisted by the local education authority.

Expenses.

32.—(1) *There shall be paid out of moneys provided by Parliament any expenditure incurred by any Minister under or by virtue of this Act.*   5

(2) *Any increase attributable to the provisions of this Act in the sums payable out of moneys provided by Parliament by way of rate-support grant under the enactments relating to local government in England and Wales shall be paid out of moneys so provided.*   10

Short title and extent.

33.—(1) This Act may be cited as the Chronically Sick and Disabled Persons Act 1969.

(2) This Act does not extend to Scotland or Northern Ireland.

Chronically Sick and Disabled Persons

A

B I L L

To make further provision with respect to the welfare of chronically sick and disabled persons; and for connected purposes.

Presented by Mr. Alfred Morris,

supported by

Mr. Jack Ashley, Dr. Shirley Summerskill, Mr. Neil Marten, Dr. Michael Winstanley, Mr. Will Griffiths, Mr. John Astor, Mrs. Lena Jeger, Mr. George Darling, Mr. Lewis Carter-Jones, Sir Clive Bossom and Mr. Laurence Pavitt

Chronically Sick and Disabled Persons Act 1970

CHAPTER 44

ARRANGEMENT OF SECTIONS

1970 CHAPTER 44

An Act to make further provision with respect to the welfare of chronically sick and disabled persons; and for connected purposes.   [29th May 1970]

B E IT ENACTED by the Queen's most Excellent Majesty, by and with the advice and consent of the Lords Spiritual and Temporal, and Commons, in this present Parliament assembled, and by the authority of the same, as follows:—

Welfare and housing

1.—(1) It shall be the duty of every local authority having functions under section 29 of the National Assistance Act 1948 to inform themselves of the number of persons to whom that section applies within their area and of the need for the making by the authority of arrangements under that section for such persons.

Information as to need for and existence of welfare services.

1948 c. 29.

(2) Every such local authority—

> (*a*) shall cause to be published from time to time at such times and in such manner as they consider appropriate general information as to the services provided under arrangements made by the authority under the said section 29 which are for the time being available in their area; and

> (*b*) shall ensure that any such person as aforesaid who uses any of those services is informed of any other of those services which in the opinion of the authority is relevant to his needs.

(3) This section shall come into operation on such date as the Secretary of State may by order made by statutory instrument appoint.

A 2

Provision of welfare services.
1948 c. 29.

2.—(1) Where a local authority having functions under section 29 of the National Assistance Act 1948 are satisfied in the case of any person to whom that section applies who is ordinarily resident in their area that it is necessary in order to meet the needs of that person for that authority to make arrangements for all or any of the following matters, namely—

(*a*) the provision of practical assistance for that person in his home;

(*b*) the provision for that person of, or assistance to that person in obtaining, wireless, television, library or similar recreational facilities;

(*c*) the provision for that person of lectures, games, outings or other recreational facilities outside his home or assistance to that person in taking advantage of educational facilities available to him;

(*d*) the provision for that person of facilities for, or assistance in, travelling to and from his home for the purpose of participating in any services provided under arrangements made by the authority under the said section 29 or, with the approval of the authority, in any services provided otherwise than as aforesaid which are similar to services which could be provided under such arrangements;

(*e*) the provision of assistance for that person in arranging for the carrying out of any works of adaptation in his home or the provision of any additional facilities designed to secure his greater safety, comfort or convenience;

(*f*) facilitating the taking of holidays by that person, whether at holiday homes or otherwise and whether provided under arrangements made by the authority or otherwise;

(*g*) the provision of meals for that person whether in his home or elsewhere;

(*h*) the provision for that person of, or assistance to that person in obtaining, a telephone and any special equipment necessary to enable him to use a telephone,

then, notwithstanding anything in any scheme made by the authority under the said section 29, but subject to the provisions of section 35(2) of that Act (which requires local authorities to exercise their functions under Part III of that Act under the general guidance of the Secretary of State and in accordance with the provisions of any regulations made for the purpose), it shall be the duty of that authority to make those arrangements in exercise of their functions under the said section 29.

(2) Without prejudice to the said section 35(2), subsection (3) of the said section 29 (which requires any arrangements made by

a local authority under that section to be carried into effect in accordance with a scheme made thereunder) shall not apply—

    (*a*) to any arrangements made in pursuance of subsection (1) of this section; or

    (*b*) in the case of a local authority who have made such a scheme, to any arrangements made by virtue of subsection (1) of the said section 29 in addition to those required or authorised by the scheme which are so made with the approval of the Secretary of State.

    3.—(1) Every local authority for the purposes of Part V of the Duties of Housing Act 1957 in discharging their duty under section 91 of housing that Act to consider housing conditions in their district and the authorities. needs of the district with respect to the provision of further 1957 c. 56. housing accommodation shall have regard to the special needs of chronically sick or disabled persons; and any proposals prepared and submitted to the Minister by the authority under that section for the provision of new houses shall distinguish any houses which the authority propose to provide which make special provision for the needs of such persons.

    (2) In the application of this section to Scotland for the words " Part V of the Housing Act 1957 ", " 91 " and " Minister " there shall be substituted respectively the words " Part VII of the Housing (Scotland) Act 1966 ", " 137 " and " Secretary of 1966 c. 49. State ".

Premises open to public

    4.—(1) Any person undertaking the provision of any building Access to, and or premises to which the public are to be admitted, whether on facilities at, payment or otherwise, shall, in the means of access both to and premises within the building or premises, and in the parking facilities and open to the sanitary conveniences to be available (if any), make provision, in public. so far as it is in the circumstances both practicable and reasonable, for the needs of members of the public visiting the building or premises who are disabled.

    (2) This section shall not apply to any building or premises intended for purposes mentioned in subsection (2) of section 8 of this Act.

    5.—(1) Where any local authority undertake the provision of a Provision of public sanitary convenience, it shall be the duty of the authority, in public sanitary doing so, to make provision, in so far as it is in the circumstances conveniences. both practicable and reasonable, for the needs of disabled persons.

    (2) Any local authority which in any public sanitary convenience provided by them make or have made provision for the needs of disabled persons shall take such steps as may be reasonable, by sign-posts or similar notices, to indicate the whereabouts of the convenience.

1933 c. 51.
1947 c. 43.

(3) In this section " local authority " means a local authority within the meaning of the Local Government Act 1933 or the Local Government (Scotland) Act 1947 and any joint board or joint committee of which all the constituent authorities are local authorities within the meaning of either of those Acts.

Provision of
sanitary
conveniences
at certain
premises open
to the public.
1936 c. 49.

6.—(1) Any person upon whom a notice is served with respect to any premises under section 89 of the Public Health Act 1936 (which empowers local authorities by notice to make requirements as to the provision and maintenance of sanitary conveniences for the use of persons frequenting certain premises used for the accommodation, refreshment or entertainment of members of the public) shall in complying with that notice make provision, in so far as it is in the circumstances both practicable and reasonable, for the needs of persons frequenting those premises who are disabled.

1959 c. 24.

(2) The owner of a building, who has been ordered under section 11(4) of the Building (Scotland) Act 1959 to make the building conform to a provision of building standards regulations made under section 3 of that Act requiring the provision of suitable and sufficient sanitary conveniences therein, shall in complying with that order make provision, in so far as it is in the circumstances both practicable and reasonable, for the needs of persons frequenting that building who are disabled.

Signs at
buildings
complying
with ss. 4–6.

7.—(1) Where any provision required by or under section 4, 5 or 6 of this Act is made at a building in compliance with that section, a notice or sign indicating that provision is made for the disabled shall be displayed outside the building or so as to be visible from outside it.

(2) This section applies to a sanitary convenience provided elsewhere than in a building, and not itself being a building, as it applies to a building.

University and school buildings

Access to, and
facilities at,
university
and school
buildings.

8.—(1) Any person undertaking the provision of a building intended for purposes mentioned in subsection (2) below shall, in the means of access both to and within the building, and in the parking facilities and sanitary conveniences to be available (if any), make provision, in so far as it is in the circumstances both practicable and reasonable, for the needs of persons using the building who are disabled.

(2) The purposes referred to in subsection (1) above are the purposes of any of the following:—

    (*a*) universities, university colleges and colleges, schools and halls of universities;

(*b*) schools within the meaning of the Education Act 1944, 1944 c. 31. teacher training colleges maintained by local education authorities in England or Wales and other institutions providing further education pursuant to a scheme under section 42 of that Act;

(*c*) educational establishments within the meaning of the Education (Scotland) Act 1962.   1962 c. 37.

Advisory committees, etc.

9.—(1) The Secretary of State shall ensure that the central Central advisory committee constituted under section 3 of the War advisory Pensions Act 1921 includes the chairmen of not less than twelve committee of the committees established by schemes under section 1 of that pensions. Act and includes at least one war disabled pensioner, and shall 1921 c. 49. cause that central advisory committee to be convened at least once in every year.

(2) This section extends to Northern Ireland.

10. In the appointment of persons to be members of the Central Housing Housing Advisory Committee set up under section 143 of the Advisory Housing Act 1957 or of the Scottish Housing Advisory Committee Committees. set up under section 167 of the Housing (Scotland) Act 1966, 1957 c. 56. regard shall be had to the desirability of that Committee's 1966 c. 49. including one or more persons with knowledge of the problems involved in housing the chronically sick and disabled and to the person or persons with that knowledge being or including a chronically sick or disabled person or persons.

11. The National Insurance Advisory Committee shall include National at least one person with experience of work among and of the Insurance needs of the chronically sick and disabled and in selecting any Advisory such person regard shall be had to the desirability of having a Committee. chronically sick or disabled person.

12. The Industrial Injuries Advisory Council shall include at Industrial least one person with experience of work among and of the Injuries needs of the chronically sick and disabled and in selecting any Advisory such person regard shall be had to the desirability of having a Council. chronically sick or disabled person.

13.—(1) Without prejudice to any other arrangements that Youth may be made by the Secretary of State, the Central Youth employment Employment Executive shall include at least one person with service. special responsibility for the employment of young disabled persons.

(2) In the appointment of persons to be members of any of the bodies constituted in pursuance of section 8(1) of the Employ- ment and Training Act 1948 (that is to say, the National Youth 1948 c. 46.

Employment Council and the Advisory Committees on Youth Employment for Scotland and Wales respectively) regard shall be had to the desirability of the body in question including one or more persons with experience of work among, and the special needs of, young disabled persons and to the person or persons with that experience being or including a disabled person or persons.

Miscellaneous advisory committees.

14.—(1) In the appointment of persons to be members of any of the following advisory committees or councils, that is to say, the Transport Users' Consultative Committees, the Gas Consultative Councils, the Electricity Consultative Councils, the Post Office Users' Councils and the Domestic Coal Consumers' Council, regard shall be had to the desirability of the committee or council in question including one or more persons with experience of work among, and the special needs of, disabled persons and to the person or persons with that experience being or including a disabled person or persons.

(2) In this section the reference to the Post Office Users' Councils is a reference to the Councils established under section 14 of the Post Office Act 1969, and in relation to those Councils this section shall extend to Northern Ireland.

1969 c. 48.

Co-option of chronically sick or disabled persons to local authority committees.
1933 c. 51.
1947 c. 43.

15. Where a local authority within the meaning of the Local Government Act 1933 or the Local Government (Scotland) Act 1947 appoint a committee of the authority under any enactment, and the members of the committee include or may include persons who are not members of the authority, then in considering the appointment to the committee of such persons regard shall be had, if the committee is concerned with matters in which the chronically sick or disabled have special needs, to the desirability of appointing to the committee persons with experience of work among and of the needs of the chronically sick and disabled, and to the person or persons with that experience being or including a chronically sick or disabled person or persons.

Duties of national advisory council under Disabled Persons (Employment) Act 1944.
1944 c. 10.

16. The duties of the national advisory council established under section 17(1)(*a*) of the Disabled Persons (Employment) Act 1944 shall include in particular the duty of giving to the Secretary of State such advice as appears to the council to be necessary on the training of persons concerned with—

(*a*) placing disabled persons in employment; or

(*b*) training disabled persons for employment.

Provisions with respect to persons under 65

17.—(1) Every Board constituted under section 11 of the National Health Service Act 1946 ('hat is to say, every Regional Hospital Board and every Board of Governors of a teaching hospital) and every Regional Hospital Board constituted under section 11 of the National Health Service (Scotland) Act 1947 shall use their best endeavours to secure that, so far as practicable, in any hospital for which they are responsible a person who is suffering from a condition of chronic illness or disability and who—

Separation of
younger from
older patients.

1946 c. 81.

1947 c. 27.

> (a) is in the hospital for the purpose of long-term care for that condition; or
>
> (b) normally resides elsewhere but is being cared for in the hospital because—
>
> > (i) that condition is such as to preclude him from residing elsewhere without the assistance of some other person; and
> >
> > (ii) such assistance is for the time being not available,

is not cared for in the hospital as an in-patient in any part of the hospital which is normally used wholly or mainly for the care of elderly persons, unless he is himself an elderly person.

(2) Each such Board as aforesaid shall provide the Secretary of State in such form and at such times as he may direct with such information as he may from time to time require as to any persons to whom subsection (1) of this section applied who, not being elderly persons, have been cared for in any hospital for which that Board are responsible in such a part of the hospital as is mentioned in that subsection; and the Secretary of State shall in each year lay before each House of Parliament such statement in such form as he considers appropriate of the information obtained by him under this subsection.

(3) In this section " elderly person " means a person who is aged sixty-five or more or is suffering from the effects of premature ageing.

18.—(1) The Secretary of State shall take steps to obtain from local authorities having functions under Part III of the National Assistance Act 1948 information as to the number of persons under the age of 65 appearing to the local authority in question to be persons to whom section 29 of that Act applies for whom residential accommodation is from time to time provided under section 21(1)(a) or 26(1)(a) of that Act at any premises in a part of those premises in which such accommodation is so provided for persons over that age.

Information
as to accom-
modation
of younger
with older
persons under
Part III of
National
Assistance
Act 1948.

1948 c. 29.

1968 c. 49.

1960 c. 61.

(2) The Secretary of State shall take steps to obtain from local authorities having functions under the Social Work (Scotland) Act 1968 information as to the number of persons under the age of 65 who suffer from illness or mental disorder within the meaning of section 6 of the Mental Health (Scotland) Act 1960 or are substantially handicapped by any deformity or disability and for whom residential accommodation is from time to time provided under section 59 of the said Act of 1968 at any premises in a part of those premises in which such accommodation is so provided for persons over that age.

(3) Every local authority referred to in this section shall provide the Secretary of State in such form and at such times as he may direct with such information as he may from time to time require for the purpose of this section; and the Secretary of State shall in each year lay before each House of Parliament such statement in such form as he considers appropriate of the information obtained by him under this section.

Provision of information relating to chiropody services.

1968 c. 46.

1947 c. 27.

19. Every local health authority empowered to provide chiropody services under section 12 of the Health Services and Public Health Act 1968, or under section 27 of the National Health Service (Scotland) Act 1947, shall provide the Secretary of State in such form and at such times as he may direct with information as to the extent to which those services are available and used for the benefit of disabled persons under the age of sixty-five.

Miscellaneous provisions

Use of invalid carriages on highways.

20.—(1) In the case of a vehicle which is an invalid carriage complying with the prescribed requirements and which is being used in accordance with the prescribed conditions—

(*a*) no statutory provision prohibiting or restricting the use of footways shall prohibit or restrict the use of that vehicle on a footway;

1960 c. 16.
1962 c. 59.
1967 c. 76.
1967 c. 30.

(*b*) if the vehicle is mechanically propelled, it shall be treated for the purposes of the Road Traffic Act 1960, the Road Traffic Act 1962, the Road Traffic Regulation Act 1967 and Part I of the Road Safety Act 1967 as not being a motor vehicle; and

1957 c. 51.

(*c*) whether or not the vehicle is mechanically propelled, it shall be exempted from the requirements of the Road Transport Lighting Act 1957.

(2) In this section—

1959 c. 25.

" footway " means a way which is a footway, footpath or bridleway within the meaning of the Highways Act 1959;

and in its application to Scotland means a way over which the public has a right of passage on foot only or a bridleway within the meaning of section 47 of the Countryside (Scotland) Act 1967;   1967 c. 86.

" invalid carriage " means a vehicle, whether mechanically propelled or not, constructed or adapted for use for the carriage of one person, being a person suffering from some physical defect or disability;

" prescribed " means prescribed by regulations made by the Minister of Transport;

" statutory provision " means a provision contained in, or having effect under, any enactment.

(3) Any regulations made under this section shall be made by statutory instrument, may make different provision for different circumstances and shall be subject to annulment in pursuance of a resolution of either House of Parliament.

21.—(1) There shall be a badge of a prescribed form to be issued by local authorities for motor vehicles driven by, or used for the carriage of, disabled persons; and— *Badges for display on motor vehicles used by disabled persons.*

(a) subject to the provisions of this section, the badge so issued for any vehicle or vehicles may be displayed on it or on any of them either inside or outside the area of the issuing authority; and

(b) any power under section 84C of the Road Traffic Regulation Act 1967 (which was inserted by the Transport Act 1968) to make regulations requiring that orders under the Act shall include exemptions shall be taken to extend to requiring that an exemption given with reference to badges issued by one authority shall be given also with reference to badges issued by other authorities.   *1967 c. 76. 1968 c. 73.*

(2) A badge may be issued to a disabled person of any prescribed description resident in the area of the issuing authority for one or more vehicles which he drives and, if so issued, may be displayed on it or any of them at times when he is the driver.

(3) In such cases as may be prescribed, a badge may be issued to a disabled person of any prescribed description so resident for one or more vehicles used by him as a passenger and, if so issued, may be displayed on it or any of them at times when the vehicle is being used to carry him.

A badge may be issued to the same person both under this subsection and under subsection (2) above.

(4) A badge may be issued to an institution concerned with the care of the disabled for any motor vehicle or, as the case

may be, for each motor vehicle kept in the area of the issuing authority and used by or on behalf of the institution to carry disabled persons of any prescribed description; and any badge so issued may be displayed on the vehicle for which it is issued at times when the vehicle is being so used.

(5) A local authority shall maintain a register showing the holders of badges issued by the authority under this section, and the vehicle or vehicles for which each of the badges is held; and in the case of badges issued to disabled persons the register shall show whether they were, for any motor vehicle, issued under subsection (2) or under subsection (3) or both.

(6) A badge issued under this section shall remain the property of the issuing authority, shall be issued for such period as may be prescribed, and shall be returned to the issuing authority in such circumstances as may be prescribed.

(7) Anything which is under this section to be prescribed shall be prescribed by regulations made by the Minister of Transport and Secretary of State by statutory instrument, which shall be, subject to annulment in pursuance of a resolution of either House of Parliament; and regulations so made may make provision—

(*a*) as to the cases in which authorities may refuse to issue badges, and as to the fee (if any) which an authority may charge for the issue or re-issue of a badge; and

(*b*) as to the continuing validity or effect of badges issued before the coming into force of this section in pursuance of any scheme having effect under section 29 of the National Assistance Act 1948 or any similar scheme having effect in Scotland; and

1948 c. 29.

(*c*) as to any transitional matters, and in particular the application to badges issued under this section of orders made before it comes into force and operating with reference to any such badges as are referred to in paragraph (*b*) above (being orders made, or having effect as if made, under the Road Traffic Regulation Act 1967).

1967 c. 76.

(8) The local authorities for purposes of this section shall be the common council of the City of London, the council of a county or county borough in England or Wales or of a London borough and the council of a county or large burgh in Scotland; and in this section " motor vehicle " has the same meaning as in the Road Traffic Regulation Act 1967.

(9) This section shall come into operation on such date as the Minister of Transport and Secretary of State may by order made by statutory instrument appoint.

22. The Secretary of State shall as respects each year lay before Parliament a report on the progress made during that year in research and development work carried out by or on behalf of any Minister of the Crown in relation to equipment that might increase the range of activities and independence or well-being of disabled persons, and in particular such equipment that might improve the indoor and outdoor mobility of such persons. Annual report on research and development work.

23.—(1) The Pensions Appeal Tribunals Act 1943 shall have effect with the amendments specified in the subsequent provisions of this section. War pensions appeals. 1943 c. 39.

(2) In section 5—

(a) so much of subsection (1) as prevents the making of an appeal from an interim assessment of the degree of a disablement before the expiration of two years from the first notification of the making of an interim assessment (that is to say, the words from " if " to " subsection " where first occurring, and the words " in force at the expiration of the said period of two years ") is hereby repealed except in relation to a claim in the case of which the said first notification was given before the commencement of this Act;

(b) in the second paragraph of subsection (1) (which defines " interim assessment " for the purposes of that subsection), for the words " this subsection " there shall be substituted the words " this section ";

(c) in subsection (2) (which provides for an appeal to a tribunal from a Ministerial decision or assessment purporting to be a final settlement of a claim) at the end there shall be added the words " and if the Tribunal so set aside the Minister's decision or assessment they may, if they think fit, make such interim assessment of the degree or nature of the disablement, to be in force until such date not later than two years after the making of the Tribunal's assessment, as they think proper ";

(d) subsection (3) (which makes provision as to the coming into operation of section 5) is hereby repealed.

(3) In section 6, after subsection (2) there shall be inserted the following subsection—

" (2A) Where, in the case of such a claim as is referred to in section 1, 2, 3 or 4 of this Act—

(a) an appeal has been made under that section to the Tribunal and that appeal has been decided (whether with or without an appeal under subsection (2) of this section from the Tribunal's decision); but

12   c. **44**   *Chronically Sick and Disabled Persons Act 1970*

(*b*) subsequently, on an application for the purpose made (in like manner as an application for leave to appeal under the said subsection (2)) jointly by the appellant and the Minister, it appears to the appropriate authority (that is to say, the person to whom under rules made under the Schedule to this Act any application for directions on any matter arising in connection with the appeal to the Tribunal fell to be made) to be proper so to do—

(i) by reason of the availability of additional evidence; or

(ii) (except where an appeal from the Tribunal's decision has been made under the said subsection (2)), on the ground of the Tribunal's decision being erroneous in point of law,

the appropriate authority may, if he thinks fit, direct that the decision on the appeal to the Tribunal be treated as set aside and the appeal from the Minister's decision be heard again by the Tribunal ".

(4) In subsection (3) of section 6 (under which, subject to subsection (2) of that section, a tribunal's decision is final and conclusive) for the words " subject to the last foregoing subsection " there shall be substituted the words " subject to subsections (2) and (2A) of this section ".

S.I. 1968/1699.   (5) In consequence of the Secretary of State for Social Services Order 1968, in section 12(1), for the definition of " the Minister " there shall be substituted the following:—

" ' the Minister ' means the Secretary of State for Social Services ".

(6) This section extends to Northern Ireland.

Institute of hearing research.   **24.** The Secretary of State shall collate and present evidence to the Medical Research Council on the need for an institute for hearing research, such institute to have the general function of co-ordinating and promoting research on hearing and assistance to the deaf and hard of hearing.

Special educational treatment for the deaf-blind.   **25.**—(1) It shall be the duty of every local education authority to provide the Secretary of State at such times as he may direct with information on the provision made by that local education authority of special educational facilities for children who suffer the dual handicap of blindness and deafness.

(2) The arrangements made by a local education authority for the special educational treatment of the deaf-blind shall, so far as is practicable, provide for the giving of such education in any school maintained or assisted by the local education authority.

(3) In the application of this section to Scotland for any reference to a local education authority there shall be substituted a reference to an education authority within the meaning of section 145 of the Education (Scotland) Act 1962.   1962 c. 47.

26.—(1) It shall be the duty of every local education authority to provide the Secretary of State at such times as he may direct with information on the provision made by that local education authority of special educational facilities for children who suffer from autism or other forms of early childhood psychosis.

Special educational treatment for children suffering from autism, &c.

(2) The arrangements made by a local education authority for the special educational treatment of children suffering from autism and other forms of early childhood psychosis shall, so far as is practicable, provide for the giving of such education in any school maintained or assisted by the local education authority.

(3) In the application of this section to Scotland for any reference to a local education authority there shall be substituted a reference to an education authority within the meaning of section 145 of the Education (Scotland) Act 1962.

27.—(1) It shall be the duty of every local education authority to provide the Secretary of State at such times as he may direct with information on the provision made by that local education authority of special educational facilities for children who suffer from acute dyslexia.

Special educational treatment for children suffering from acute dyslexia.

(2) The arrangements made by a local education authority for the special educational treatment of children suffering from acute dyslexia shall, so far as is practicable, provide for the giving of such education in any school maintained or assisted by the local education authority.

(3) In the application of this section to Scotland for any reference to a local education authority there shall be substituted a reference to an education authority within the meaning of section 145 of the Education (Scotland) Act 1962.

28. Where it appears to the Secretary of State to be necessary or expedient to do so for the proper operation of any provision of this Act, he may by regulations made by statutory instrument, which shall be subject to annulment in pursuance of a resolution of either House of Parliament, make provision as to the interpretation for the purposes of that provision of any of the following expressions appearing therein, that is to say, " chronically sick ", " chronic illness ", " disabled " and " disability ".

Power to define certain expressions.

29.—(1) This Act may be cited as the Chronically Sick and Disabled Persons Act 1970.

(2) Sections 1 and 2 of this Act do not extend to Scotland.

Short title, extent and commence- ment.

Dd 0291148 K12 6/79

(3) Save as otherwise expressly provided by sections 9, 14 and 23, this Act does not extend to Northern Ireland.

(4) This Act shall come into force as follows:—

(*a*) sections 1 and 21 shall come into force on the day appointed thereunder;

(*b*) sections 4, 5, 6, 7 and 8 shall come into force at the expiration of six months beginning with the date this Act is passed;

(*c*) the remainder shall come into force at the expiration of three months beginning with that date.

Index

130023

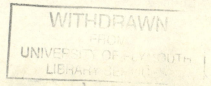

Aspects of Social Policy

General Editor:
J. P. Martin
Professor of Sociology and Social
Administration
University of Southampton

Planning for Welfare
Social Policy and the
Expenditure Process
edited by TIMOTHY A. BOOTH

Penal Policy in a Modern
Welfare State
A. E. BOTTOMS

The Social Context of
Health Care
PAUL BREARLEY, JANE GIBBONS,
AGNES MILES. EDA TOPLISS and
GRAHAM WOODS

Reserved for the Poor
The Means Test in British
Social Policy
ERIC BRIGGS and ALAN DEACON

Reorganising the National
Health Service
A Case Study in
Administrative Change
R. G. S. BROWN

Social Policy: A Survey of
Recent Developments
edited by MICHAEL H. COOPER

The Poverty Business
JOAN HIGGINS

States of Welfare
Comparative Analysis in
Social Policy
JOAN HIGGINS

Understanding Social Policy
MICHAEL HILL

Health, Wealth and
Housing
edited by R. A. B. LEAPER

The Child's Generation
Second Edition
JEAN PACKMAN

The Sociology of Welfare
GRAHAM ROOM

The Organisation of Soviet
Medical Care
MICHAEL RYAN

Provision for the Disabled
EDA TOPLISS

Alternative Strategies for
Coping with Crime
edited by NORMAN TUTT

Efficiency in the Social
Services
ALAN WILLIAMS and
ROBERT ANDERSON